D1109663

Morality and the Law

Basic Problems in Philosophy Series

A. I. Melden and Stanley Munsat
University of California, Irvine
General Editors

The Analytic-Synthetic Distinction
Stanley Munsat

Civil Disobedience and Violence
Jeffrie G. Murphy, The University of Arizona

Guilt and Shame
Herbert Morris, University of California, Los Angeles

Human Rights
A. I. Melden

Morality and the Law
Richard A. Wasserstrom, University of California, Los Angeles

War and Morality
Richard A. Wasserstrom

Morality and the Law

Edited by

Richard A. Wasserstrom
University of California, Los Angeles

Wadsworth Publishing Company, Inc.   Belmont, California

Series Foreword

The Basic Problems in Philosophy Series is designed to meet the need of students and teachers of philosophy, mainly but not exclusively at the undergraduate level, for collections of essays devoted to some fairly specific philosophical problems.

In recent years there have been numerous paperback collections on a variety of philosophical topics. Those teachers who wish to refer their students to a set of essays on a specific philosophical problem have usually been frustrated, however, since most of these collections range over a wide set of issues and problems. The present series attempts to remedy this situation by presenting together, within each volume, key writings on a single philosophical issue.

Given the magnitude of the literature, there can be no thought of completeness. Rather, the materials included are those that, in the judgment of the editor, must be mastered first by the student who wishes to acquaint himself with relevant issues and their ramifications. To this end, historical as well as contemporary writings will be included.

Each volume in the series will contain an introduction by the editor to set the stage for the arguments contained in the essays and a bibliography to help the student who wishes to pursue the topic at a more advanced level.

A. I. Melden
S. Munsat

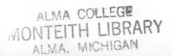

Richard Alan Wasserstrom is a professor of law and a professor of philosophy at the University of California, Los Angeles. He received a B.A. degree from Amherst College, an M.A. and a Ph.D. from the University of Michigan, and an LL.B. from Stanford University. In addition to teaching at Stanford and U.C.L.A. he has served as an attorney in the Civil Rights Division of the Justice Department and as Dean of the College of Arts and Sciences at Tuskegee Institute. During 1970–1971 he was the holder of a Guggenheim Fellowship and was a Visiting Fellow of All Souls College, Oxford. He has published two books, *The Judicial Decision* (1961) and *War and Morality* (1970), and several articles, including "The Obligation to Obey the Law," *U.C.L.A. Law Review,* Vol. 10 (1963).

Contents

Introduction

"Morality and the Law" is a phrase that only ambiguously in- **1**
dicates the area of interest central to these readings. A more
specific, but still imprecise, description is that these readings
are concerned with the question of whether the immorality of
a kind of behavior can ever, by itself, be sufficient justification
for making that kind of behavior illegal. The concern here,
therefore, is with what is fundamentally a normative issue—the
appropriateness of certain criteria as guides for the regulation of conduct by the law. On the other hand, there are several
topics which also fall appropriately under the heading "Morality and the Law" with which these readings are not directly
concerned. Thus, they are not devoted to the claim often
made by legal philosophers that there is some logical connection between the concept of law (and its cognate concepts)
and the concept of morality (and its cognate concepts).[1] Nor
are they concerned with the sociological or historical study
of the ways in which morality can affect the law or the law
can affect morality.

The philosophical problem at hand has acquired a name of
its own: "the enforcement of morals by the law." Like a number of other philosophical problems, it has also had something
of a life of its own. Hence, another way to develop a clearer
sense of the topic to which these readings are addressed
is to examine the history of this particular philosophical
problem.

For our purposes, then, history begins with the publication
of John Stuart Mill's essay, *On Liberty,* in 1859. The question
which Mill put to himself to answer in this essay was of extraordinary breadth: What is the nature and what are the limits
of the power which can be legitimately exercised by society
over the individual?

*The object of this Essay is to assert one very simple prin-
ciple, as entitled to govern absolutely the dealings of society
with the individual in the way of compulsion and control,*

---

[1] Among the key contemporary sources on this topic are: Hans Kelsen,
General Theory of Law and the State (1945); H. L. A. Hart, *The Concept of
Law* (1961); and Lon L. Fuller, *The Morality of Law* (1963, revised ed., 1969).

whether the means used be physical force in the form of legal penalties, or the moral coercion of public opinion. That principle is, that the sole end for which mankind are warranted, individually or collectively, in interfering with the liberty of action of any of their number, is self-protection. That the only purpose for which power can be rightfully exercised over any member of a civilized community, against his will, is to prevent harm to others. His own good, either physical or moral, is not a sufficient warrant. He cannot rightfully be compelled to do or forbear because it will be better for him to do so, because it will make him happier, because, in the opinions of others, to do so would be wise, or even right. . . .[2]

Having laid down this general principle (or set of principles), Mill went on to examine in more detail the supporting arguments for and specific applications of this principle. His defense of the principle rested first upon a conception of what it was to develop most adequately or fully one's characteristics as a person, and second upon a view of what conditions were most conducive to that development. Thus, Mill was led to emphasize, in a famous portion of the essay, the importance of freedom of thought and discussion. At the conclusion of this analysis and an analysis of the nature of individuality, he turned more directly to a consideration of how these notions affect our understanding of the legitimate areas of societal control over the individual. Almost all of this portion of the essay constitutes the first selection of this collection.[3]

Mill was not without his critics, even in his own time. The most famous of his contemporary opponents was Sir James Fitzjames Stephen, a distinguished historian and commentator upon the criminal law. Fourteen years after the appearance of *On Liberty*, Stephen's book, *Liberty, Equality, Fraternity*, was published. Its expressed central objective was to refute the fundamental theses of *On Liberty*. Stephen's criticism of Mill was that the inappropriate uses of compulsion by society upon an individual could not be determined simply by deciding whether the individual's conduct was harmful to others. "To me," said Stephen, "the question whether liberty is a good or a bad thing appears as irrational as the question whether fire is a good or a bad thing. It is both good and bad according to time, place, and circumstance . . ."[4]

2 J. S. Mill, *On Liberty*, Chapter 1.
3 Pp. 10–23 below.
4 Stephen, *Liberty, Equality, Fraternity*, p. 48.

"If . . . the object aimed at is good, if the compulsion employed such as to attain it, and if the good obtained overbalances the inconvenience of the compulsion itself, I do not understand how, upon utilitarian principles, the compulsion can be bad."[5] This applies, Stephen argued, both to the regulation of thought and discussion and to the regulation of morals, whether undertaken by public opinion or by the law. In particular, insisted Stephen, in the area of immoral behavior, the punishment of the grosser forms of vice constituted as legitimate an objective as did the prevention of harm to others.

There the matter rested until the period shortly after the Second World War. At that time, events in England and the United States generated a renewed interest in the basic Millian thesis and in the areas to which it should be applied.

In August of 1954, in England, a committee under the chairmanship of John Wolfenden was established to consider the existing English penal laws concerning homosexuality and prostitution and to recommend the changes, if any, to be made in those laws. In 1957 the committee issued its report, the famous Wolfenden Report. It recommended that homosexual behavior occurring in private between consenting adults no longer be punishable under the law. And the report also recommended no change in the existing law under which acts of prostitution were not in themselves illegal. In language quite reminiscent of *On Liberty,* the committee based its recommendations upon a distinction between matters of private morality (with which the criminal law ought to have no direct concern) and matters of public order, decency, and harm to others (with which the criminal law could quite properly be concerned).[6]

At roughly the same time the Wolfenden Committee was engaged in its deliberations, activity was begun in the United States to draft a model penal code. This code was prepared under the general auspices of the American Law Institute and under the specific guidance of Professor Herbert Wechsler and a small group of legal scholars, judges, and attorneys. These drafters, too, wrestled with the general problem of the appropriate limits of the criminal law and with the more specific problem of the relevance of the immorality of an action

[5] *Ibid.,* p. 50.

[6] *Report of the Committee on Homosexual Offenses and Prostitution,* paragraphs 13 and 14. (The precise language is quoted on pp. 29–30 of the essay by Lord Devlin, "Morals and the Criminal Law," which is to be found in this collection beginning on p. 24.)

to its illegality. The final recommendations of the Model Penal Code in respect to homosexuality and prostitution were very similar to those contained in the Wolfenden Report.[7]

In 1958, one hundred years after the publication of *On Liberty,* Lord Patrick Devlin delivered an important lecture to the British Academy. The lecture, entitled "The Enforcement of Morals," was offered by Lord Devlin as a criticism both of the theory on which the Wolfenden Committee's recommendations had been based and of the recommendations themselves. Because the lecture was a reply to the Wolfenden Report, it focused on the topics of homosexuality and prostitution. However, as Lord Devlin has subsequently made clear, he perceived the Report as deriving from the more pervasive Millian thesis, and he therefore regarded his attack upon the Report as a criticism of Mill's position.[8]

Lord Devlin's lecture produced within a very short time a number of replies and rebuttals, both popular and academic. One of the first to respond was H. L. A. Hart, Professor of Jurisprudence at Oxford University, whose talk "Immorality and Treason" was delivered on a program of the British Broadcasting Company in 1959. It is included in this collection on pages 49–54. Several years later, Professor Hart expanded these initial remarks into a qualified defense of Mill's thesis and a more comprehensive criticism of Lord Devlin's position. This more extended discussion appeared in a small book published in 1963, entitled *Law, Liberty and Morality.* Professor Hart disagreed with Lord Devlin and agreed with Mill on what he took to be a central point of Lord Devlin's argument: the legitimacy of making immoral conduct criminal (under certain circumstances) even if the conduct is not harmful to others. Professor Hart qualified his defense of Mill, however, by insisting that paternalism—the prevention of serious harm to the actor—furnished an independent, permissible basis upon which to make conduct illegal.[9] Because Lord Devlin had

---

[7] The Code's solution to these problems is discussed in the article by Professor Louis Schwartz which appears in this collection beginning on page 86.

[8] Lord Devlin republished his original lecture in 1965 in a collection of his essays entitled *The Enforcement of Morals.* (In the collection the name of the lecture was changed to "Morals and the Criminal Law.") In the preface to *The Enforcement of Morals,* Lord Devlin describes how he came to the views contained in the lecture, "The Enforcement of Morals." That lecture, under its new title, is reproduced here as it appears in *The Enforcement of Morals.* Several of the footnotes which reply to his critics were added by Lord Devlin between the time the lecture was first delivered and the publication of the book in 1965.

[9] The problem of paternalism as an independent, justifiable ground for

initially concerned himself with the recommendations of the Wolfenden Committee, the major point of concentration of Professor Hart's arguments was similarly the general area of sexual behavior, and homosexual conduct in particular.

Chronologically, at least, Lord Devlin had the last word. In the years after the delivery of "The Enforcement of Morals," Lord Devlin wrote and delivered additional lectures that expanded and defended the views he had originally put forward. As has already been indicated, he collected these, together with the original lecture and a preface, into the book *The Enforcement of Morals.*

The continuing debate between Lord Devlin and Professor Hart evoked additional interest among philosophers in the subject of their disagreement. The selected bibliography at the back of this volume includes only a limited number of the articles that appeared in the 1960s on the Hart-Devlin debate. Two of the most thoughtful and comprehensive discussions are included in this collection: "Lord Devlin and the Enforcement of Morals" by Ronald Dworkin,[10] and "Sins and Crimes" by A. R. Louch.[11]

Because Lord Devlin and Professor Hart responded to the underlying problems and to each other's defenses on several occasions, the topics at issue acquired not only their names but much of the form in which they chose to cast the discussion. As a result, the history of controversy over the enforcement of morals is to some degree the story of the alteration of Mill's very general claim about society and the individual into something a good deal less comprehensive. As indicated earlier, Mill's doctrine limited the occasions upon which it was permissible for society to coerce an individual to those in which the individual's behavior caused harm to others. Both the main characters in the Hart-Devlin controversy and the commentators on the dispute saw Mill's *On Liberty* as central to the issues under discussion. However, because the Wolfenden Report had provoked the initial response, the subject that tended to be the focal point of inquiry and discussion was that of the regulation of sexual behavior by the criminal law—with the paradigmatic case being private, consensual homosexual acts between adults. Thus, the fundamental issue was often described as whether the immorality of an action could alone

---

regulation by the law is explored in some detail by Professor Gerald Dworkin in his article "Paternalism." See p. 107.

[10] See p. 55.

[11] See p. 73.

be a sufficient ground for making that action illegal, and the problem, quite naturally, was often described as concerning the appropriateness of the enforcement of morality, or of morals, by the law.

As several of the authors represented in this collection indicate, an emphasis upon the regulation of sexual behavior by the law constitutes a narrowing of the scope of Mill's inquiry. More importantly, the focus upon the regulation of sexual behavior may have worked a transformation of the nature of the problem and, hence, of the solution. This is so because problems of sexual morality may be different in important respects from problems of morality generally. The reader should consider carefully the relationship between morality and sexual morality. We find appearing in the discussions of Mill from Stephen through Devlin expressions such as "morals," "morality," "immorality," "sin," and "vice." Some of these terms are stranger to our ears today than are others. All of them require careful analysis and elucidation. More directly to the point, however, what is meant by the phrase "sexual morality"? Sometimes we do refer to something called "sexual morality"; sometimes we say of someone that his or her morals are bad, or that he or she is an immoral person. What exactly do we mean? Do we mean that the person has violated some rule or norm of *sexual morality,* or do we mean that the person's sexual behavior violates some general rule or principle of *morality?* To put the question another way, are problems of sexual morality (and the corresponding predicates) simply problems of morality as applied to sexual relationships, or are problems of sexual morality *sui generis* because, for example, sexual morality is a very special, and in many ways unique, area of human concern?

How one answers this question has important consequences for an understanding and assessment of the Hart-Devlin controversy. In particular, if problems of sexual morality are to any appreciable degree *sui generis,* then the contemporary focus upon issues of sexual morality may have distorted the more general discussion of the enforcement of morality by the law. The considerations most relevant to a rational discussion of the enforcement of sexual morality by the law may not, in fact, be the considerations most significant to the enforcement of nonsexual morality by the law. A private, consensual homosexual act between adults may be a paradigmatic case of sexual immorality, while at the same time a confusing and dubious case of immorality in general. If this is so, then the emphasis on sexual morality in contemporary discussions must be noted and properly taken into account and different paradigms of the enforcement of morality must be found and considered.

To this end, the reader may wish to consider, in addition to the examples suggested by others, whether any of the following cases present different or clearer cases of the enforcement of morality by the law:

1. *Statutes prohibiting cruelty to animals*
2. *Statutes prohibiting the consumption of alcohol*
3. *Statutes prohibiting dueling*
4. *Statutes prohibiting gambling*
5. *Statutes prohibiting euthanasia*
6. *Statutes prohibiting begging*
7. *Statutes prohibiting endurance contests*
8. *Statutes prohibiting the possession or use of marijuana*

Another topic alluded to by several of the authors, but perhaps not adequately stressed by any of them, concerns what is to count as *enforcement* by the legal system. Mill, it should be recalled, phrased his proscription in terms of the exercise of power by society over the individual—a most extensive category of societal action. And clearly, Mill conceived of that power being exercised by both legal and extra-legal means (e.g. public opinion). However, when it came to the way in which the legal system would exercise power, Mill tended to talk almost exclusively about the criminal sanction. So did Stephen. And so, in the essays reproduced here, do Lord Devlin and Professor Hart. Morality can, of course, be enforced by and through the criminal law, and the awesome ways in which the penal law affects the lives of those enmeshed in it may be sufficient cause to concentrate upon it alone. Nonetheless, in considering the enforcement of morality by the law it is important to bear in mind that there are a variety of potential areas for the legal enforcement of morality.

At one place in a very famous essay, "The Path of the Law," Oliver Wendell Holmes, Jr., complained about the degree to which theorists and craftsmen of the law sought to import morality into the noncriminal aspects of the law.

The duty to keep a contract at common law means a prediction that you must pay damages if you do not keep it—and nothing else. If you commit a tort, you are liable to pay a compensatory sum. If you commit a contract, you are liable to pay a compensatory sum unless the promised event comes to

*pass, and that is all the difference. But such a mode of look-
ing at the matter stinks in the nostrils of those who think it
advantageous to get as much ethics into the law as they can.*[12]

Whether or not one agrees with Holmes' analysis of the
situation and his assessment of the desirability of "getting"
ethics into the law, it seems to be the case that nonpenal areas
of the law take matters of morality into account. Is this not, in
our own legal system, at least one plausible way to account
for the high taxes imposed upon the sale of alcohol and cigarettes, or the tax benefits bestowed upon charitable contribu-
tions? In the same way, is it not fitting to characterize as cases
of the nonpenal enforcement of morality the doctrine that
prohibits the beneficiary of a will who murders the testator
from inheriting under the will and the principle that very unfair contracts are unenforceable? The point is that any complete discussion of the enforcement of morality by the law
must keep in mind the fact that the law is more than the criminal law and enforcement occurs in ways other than through
the threatened or actual application of a penal sanction.

The four cases that appear at the end of these readings are
intended to serve at least two functions. First, they afford the
reader an opportunity to observe and examine courts attempting to grapple with concrete cases of the enforcement of
morality by the law. And second, they help, perhaps, to sub-
stantiate the claim that sexual morality generates special
problems and to demonstrate that the enforcement of morality
is not limited to the criminal law.

The case of *Shaw v. Director of Public Prosecutions*[13] is
concerned with the enforcement of sexual morality by the
criminal law. It is of particular interest both because it is a
case of nonstatutory criminal enforcement and because the
opinion of Viscount Simonds invokes arguments that are much
like Lord Devlin's.

People v. Cohen[14] may or may not be about sexual morality.
In reading the case the reader should ask what there is about
the language in question that leads the court to remove it
from the protection characteristically accorded speech and
the expression of ideas. Is it the sexual connotation of the
language? Its "offensiveness"? Is the statute under which

---

[12] Holmes, "The Path of the Law," *Harvard Law Review*, Vol. 10 (1897),
p. 457.

[13] P. 127.

[14] P. 132.

Cohen was prosecuted and convicted an illustration of the enforcement of sexual morality, an example of paternalism, a case of the prevention of harm to others, or something else? If one has difficulty in answering this question in a straight-forward manner, this should suggest that the characterization of laws (e.g. as cases of the enforcement of morality) is a more complicated and ambiguous undertaking than has so far been supposed.

Repouille v. United States[15] is offered as a case of the non-penal enforcement of nonsexual morality, and *Commonwealth v. Donoghue*[16] is included as an example of the penal enforce-ment of nonsexual morality.

Hopefully, the four cases will stimulate the reader to explore the respects in which the cases are similar and the respects in which they differ in important ways. They should also serve as a quite concrete reminder that the way these philosophical issues are resolved has genuine consequences in the real world for large numbers of human beings.

---

[15] P. 140.
[16] P. 145.

John Stuart Mill

On Liberty

IV. Of the Limits to the Authority of Society over the Individual

10   What, then, is the rightful limit to the sovereignty of the individual over himself? Where does the authority of society begin? How much of human life should be assigned to individuality, and how much to society?

Each will receive its proper share, if each has that which more particularly concerns it. To individuality should belong the part of life in which it is chiefly the individual that is interested; to society, the part which chiefly interests society.

Though society is not founded on a contract, and though no good purpose is answered by inventing a contract in order to deduce social obligations from it, every one who receives the protection of society owes a return for the benefit, and the fact of living in society renders it indispensable that each should be found to observe a certain line of conduct towards the rest. This conduct consists, first, in not injuring the interests of one another; or rather certain interests, which, either by express legal provision or by tacit understanding, ought to be considered as rights; and secondly, in each person's bearing his share (to be fixed on some equitable principle) of the labours and sacrifices incurred for defending the society or its members from injury and molestation. These conditions society is justified in enforcing, at all costs to those who endeavour to withhold fulfilment. Nor is this all that society may do. The acts of an individual may be hurtful to others, or wanting in due consideration for their welfare, without going the length of violating any of their constituted rights. The offender may then be justly punished by opinion, though not by law. As soon as any part of a person's conduct affects prejudicially the interests of others, society has jurisdiction over it, and the question whether the general welfare will or will not be promoted by interfering with it, becomes open to discussion. But there is no room for entertaining any such question when a person's conduct affects the interests of no persons besides himself, or needs not affect them unless they like (all the persons concerned being of full age, and the ordinary amount of understanding). In all such cases there should be perfect freedom, legal and social, to do the action and stand the consequences.

It would be a great misunderstanding of this doctrine, to suppose that it is one of selfish indifference, which pretends that human beings have no business with each other's conduct in life, and that they should not concern themselves about the well-doing or well-being of one another, unless their own interest is involved. Instead of any diminution, there is need of a great increase of disinterested exertion to promote the good of others. But disinterested benevolence can find other instruments to persuade people to their good, than whips and scourges, either of the literal or the metaphorical sort. I am the last person to undervalue the self-regarding virtues; they are only second in importance, if even second, to the social. It is equally the business of education to cultivate both. But even education works by conviction and persuasion as well as by compulsion, and it is by the former only that, when the period of education is past, the self-regarding virtues should be inculcated. Human beings owe to each other help to distinguish the better from the worse, and encouragement to choose the former and avoid the latter. They should be for ever stimulating each other to increased exercise of their higher faculties, and increased direction of their feelings and aims towards wise instead of foolish, elevating instead of degrading, objects and contemplations. But neither one person, nor any number of persons, is warranted in saying to another human creature of ripe years, that he shall not do with his life for his own benefit what he chooses to do with it. He is the person most interested in his own well-being: the interest which any other person, except in cases of strong personal attachment, can have in it, is trifling, compared with that which he himself has; the interest which society has in him individually (except as to his conduct to others) is fractional, and altogether indirect: while, with respect to his own feelings and circumstances, the most ordinary man or woman has means of knowledge immeasurably surpassing those that can be possessed by any one else. The interference of society to overrule his judgment and purposes in what only regards himself, must be grounded on general presumptions: which may be altogether wrong, and even if right, are as likely as not to be misapplied to individual cases, by persons no better acquainted with the circumstances of such cases than those are who look at them merely from without. In this department, therefore, of human affairs, individuality has its proper field of action. In the conduct of human beings towards one another, it is necessary that general rules should for the most part be observed, in order that people may know what they have to expect; but in each person's own concerns, his individual spontaneity is entitled to free exercise. Considerations to aid his judgment, exhortations to strengthen his will, may be offered to him, even obtruded on him, by others; but he himself is the final judge. All errors which he is likely to commit against advice and warning, are far outweighed by the evil of allowing others to constrain him to what they deem his good.

I do not mean that the feelings with which a person is regarded by others, ought not to be in any way affected by his self-regarding qualities or deficiencies. This is neither possible nor desirable. If he is eminent in any of the qualities which conduce to his own good, he is, so far, a proper object of admiration. He is so much the nearer to the ideal perfection of human nature. If he is grossly deficient in those qualities, a sentiment the opposite of admiration will follow. There is a degree of folly, and a degree of what may be called (though the phrase is not unobjectionable) lowness or depravation of taste, which, though it cannot justify doing harm to the person who manifests it, renders him necessarily and properly a subject of distaste, or, in extreme cases, even of contempt: a person could not have the opposite qualities in due strength without entertaining these feelings. Though doing no wrong to any one, a person may so act as to compel us to judge him, and feel to him, as a fool, or as a being of an inferior order: and since this judgment and feeling are a fact which he would prefer to avoid, it is doing him a service to warn him of it beforehand, as of any other disagreeable consequence to which he exposes himself. It would be well, indeed, if this good office were much more freely rendered than the common notions of politeness at present permit, and if one person could honestly point out to another that he thinks him in fault, without being considered unmannerly or presuming. We have a right, also, in various ways, to act upon our unfavourable opinion of any one, not to the oppression of his individuality, but in the exercise of ours. We are not bound, for example, to seek his society; we have a right to avoid it (though not to parade the avoidance), for we have a right to choose the society most acceptable to us. We have a right, and it may be our duty, to caution others against him, if we think his example or conversation likely to have a pernicious effect on those with whom he associates. We may give others a preference over him in optional good offices, except those which tend to his improvement. In these various modes a person may suffer very severe penalties at the hands of others, for faults which directly concern only himself; but he suffers these penalties only in so far as they are the natural and, as it were, the spontaneous consequences of the faults themselves, not because they are purposely inflicted on him for the sake of punishment. A person who shows rashness, obstinacy, self-conceit—who cannot live within moderate means—who cannot restrain himself from hurtful indulgences—who pursues animal pleasures at the expense of those of feeling and intellect—must expect to be lowered in the opinion of others, and to have a less share of their favourable sentiments; but of this he has no right to complain, unless he has merited their favour by special excellence in his social relations, and has thus established a title to their good offices, which is not affected by his demerits towards himself.

What I contend for is, that the inconveniences which are strictly inseparable from the unfavourable judgment of others, are the only ones to which a person should ever be subjected for that portion of his conduct and character which concerns his own good, but which does not affect the interests of others in their relations with him. Acts injurious to others require a totally different treatment. Encroachment on their rights; infliction on them of any loss or damage not justified by his own rights; falsehood or duplicity in dealing with them; unfair or ungenerous use of advantages over them; even selfish abstinence from defending them against injury—these are fit objects of moral reprobation, and, in grave cases, of moral retribution and punishment. And not only these acts, but the dispositions which lead to them, are properly immoral, and fit subjects of disapprobation which may rise to abhorrence. Cruelty of disposition; malice and ill-nature; that most anti-social and odious of all passions, envy; dissimulation and insincerity; irascibility on insufficient cause, and resentment disproportioned to the provocation; the love of domineering over others; the desire to engross more than one's share of advantages (the πλεονεξία of the Greeks); the pride which derives gratification from the abasement of others; the egotism which thinks self and its concerns more important than everything else, and decides all doubtful questions in its own favour—these are moral vices, and constitute a bad and odious moral character: unlike the self-regarding faults previously mentioned which are not properly immoralities, and to whatever pitch they may be carried, do not constitute wickedness. They may be proofs of any amount of folly, or want of personal dignity and self-respect; but they are only a subject of moral reprobation when they involve a breach of duty to others, for whose sake the individual is bound to have care for himself. What are called duties to ourselves are not socially obligatory, unless circumstances render them at the same time duties to others. The term duty to oneself, when it means anything more than prudence, means self-respect or self-development; and for none of these is any one accountable to his fellow creatures, because for none of them is it for the good of mankind that he be held accountable to them.

The distinction between the loss of consideration which a person may rightly incur by defect of prudence or of personal dignity, and the reprobation which is due to him for an offence against the rights of others, is not a merely nominal distinction. It makes a vast difference both in our feelings and in our conduct towards him, whether he displeases us in things in which we think we have a right to control him, or in things in which we know that we have not. If he displeases us, we may express our distaste, and we may stand aloof from a person as well as from a thing that displeases us; but we shall not therefore feel called on to make his life uncomfortable. We shall reflect that he already bears, or will bear, the whole penalty of his error; if he spoils his life by mismanagement, we shall not, for that reason, desire to spoil it still further: instead of wishing to punish him, we shall rather endeavour to alleviate his punishment, by showing him how he may avoid or cure the evils his conduct tends to bring upon him. He may be to us an object of pity, perhaps of dislike, but not of anger or resentment: we shall not treat him like an enemy of society: the worst we shall think ourselves justified in doing is leaving him to himself, if we do not interfere benevolently by showing interest or concern for him. It is far otherwise if he has infringed the rules necessary for the protection of his fellow-creatures, individually or collectively. The evil consequences of his acts do not then fall on himself, but on others; and society, as the protector of all its members, must retaliate on him; must inflict pain on him for the express purpose of punishment, and must take care that it be sufficiently severe. In the one case, he is an offender at our bar, and we are called on not only to sit in judgment on him, but, in one shape or another, to execute our own sentence: in the other case, it is not our part to inflict any suffering on him, except what may incidentally follow from our using the same

liberty in the regulation of our own affairs, which we allow
to him in his.

The distinction here pointed out between the part of a
person's life which concerns only himself, and that which concerns others, many persons will refuse to admit. How (it may
be asked) can any part of the conduct of a member of society
be a matter of indifference to the other members? No person
is an entirely isolated being; it is impossible for a person to
do anything seriously or permanently hurtful to himself, without mischief reaching at least to his near connexions, and
often far beyond them. If he injures his property, he does
harm to those who directly or indirectly derived support from
it, and usually diminishes, by a greater or less amount, the
general resources of the community. If he deteriorates his
bodily or mental faculties, he not only brings evil upon all
who depended on him for any portion of their happiness, but
disqualifies himself for rendering the services which he owes
to his fellow creatures generally; perhaps becomes a burthen
on their affection or benevolence; and if such conduct were
very frequent, hardly any offence that is committed would
detract more from the general sum of good. Finally, if by his
vices or follies a person does no direct harm to others, he is
nevertheless (it may be said) injurious by his example; and
ought to be compelled to control himself, for the sake of
those whom the sight or knowledge of his conduct might corrupt or mislead.

And even (it will be added) if the consequences of misconduct could be confined to the vicious or thoughtless individual,
ought society to abandon to their own guidance those who
are manifestly unfit for it? If protection against themselves is
confessedly due to children and persons under age, is not
society equally bound to afford it to persons of mature years
who are equally incapable of self-government? If gambling,
or drunkenness, or incontinence, or idleness, or uncleanliness,
are as injurious to happiness, and as great a hindrance to
improvement, as many or most of the acts prohibited by law,
why (it may be asked) should not law, so far as is consistent
with practicability and social convenience, endeavour to repress these also? And as a supplement to the unavoidable
imperfections of law, ought not opinion at least to organize
a powerful police against these vices, and visit rigidly with
social penalties those who are known to practise them? There
is no question here (it may be said) about restricting individuality, or impeding the trial of new and original experiments
in living. The only things it is sought to prevent are things

which have been tried and condemned from the beginning of the world until now; things which experience has shown not to be useful or suitable to any person's individuality. There must be some length of time and amount of experience, after which a moral or prudential truth may be regarded as established: and it is merely desired to prevent generation after generation from falling over the same precipice which has been fatal to their predecessors.

I fully admit that the mischief which a person does to himself, may seriously affect, both through their sympathies and their interests, those nearly connected with him, and in a minor degree, society at large. When, by conduct of this sort, a person is led to violate a distinct and assignable obligation to any other person or persons, the case is taken out of the self-regarding class, and becomes amenable to moral disapprobation in the proper sense of the term. If, for example, a man, through intemperance or extravagance, becomes unable to pay his debts, or, having undertaken the moral responsibility of a family, becomes from the same cause incapable of supporting or educating them, he is deservedly reprobated, and might be justly punished; but it is for the breach of duty to his family or creditors, not for the extravagance. If the resources which ought to have been devoted to them, had been diverted from them for the most prudent investment, the moral culpability would have been the same. George Barnwell murdered his uncle to get money for his mistress, but if he had done it to set himself up in business, he would equally have been hanged. Again, in the frequent case of a man who causes grief to his family by addiction to bad habits, he deserves reproach for his unkindness or ingratitude; but so he may for cultivating habits not in themselves vicious, if they are painful to those with whom he passes his life, or who from personal ties are dependent on him for their comfort. Whoever fails in the consideration generally due to the interests and feelings of others, not being compelled by some more imperative duty, or justified by allowable self-preference, is a subject of moral disapprobation for that failure, but not for the cause of it, nor for the errors, merely personal to himself, which may have remotely led to it. In like manner, when a person disables himself, by conduct purely self-regarding, from the performance of some definite duty incumbent on him to the public, he is guilty of a social offence. No person ought to be punished simply for being drunk; but a soldier or a policeman should be punished for being drunk on duty. Whenever, in short, there is a definite damage, or a definite risk of damage, either to an individual or to the public, the case is taken out of the province of liberty, and placed in that of morality or law.

But with regard to the merely contingent, or, as it may be called, constructive injury which a person causes to society, by conduct which neither violates any specific duty to the public, nor occasions perceptible hurt to any assignable individual except himself; the inconvenience is one which society can afford to bear, for the sake of the greater good of human freedom. If grown persons are to be punished for not taking proper care of themselves, I would rather it were for their own sake, than under pretence of preventing them from impairing their capacity of rendering to society benefits which society does not pretend it has a right to exact. But I cannot consent to argue the point as if society had no means of bringing its weaker members up to its ordinary standard of rational conduct, except waiting till they do something irrational, and then punishing them, legally or morally, for it. Society has had absolute power over them during all the early portion of their existence: it has had the whole period of childhood and nonage in which to try whether it could make them capable of rational conduct in life. The existing generation is master both of the training and the entire circumstances of the generation to come; it cannot indeed make them perfectly wise and good, because it is itself so lamentably deficient in goodness and wisdom; and its best efforts are not always, in individual cases, its most successful ones; but it is perfectly well able to make the rising generation, as a whole, as good as, and a little better than, itself. If society lets any considerable number of its members grow up mere children, incapable of being acted on by rational consideration of distant motives, society has itself to blame for the consequences. Armed not only with all the powers of education, but with the ascendancy which the authority of a received opinion always exercises over the minds who are least fitted to judge for themselves; and aided by the *natural* penalties which cannot be prevented from falling on those who incur the distaste or the contempt of those who know them; let not society pretend that it needs, besides all this, the power to issue commands and enforce obedience in the personal concerns of individuals, in which, on all principles of justice and policy, the decision ought to rest with those who are to abide the consequences. Nor is there anything which tends more to discredit and frustrate the better means of influencing conduct, than a resort to the worse. If there be among those whom it is attempted to coerce into prudence or temperance, any of the material of which vigorous and independent characters are made, they will infallibly rebel against the yoke. No such person will ever feel that others have a right to control him in his concerns, such as they have to prevent him from injuring them in theirs; and it easily comes to be considered a mark of spirit and courage to fly in the face of such usurped authority, and do with ostentation the exact opposite of what it enjoins; as in the fashion of grossness which succeeded, in the time of Charles II, to the fanatical moral intolerance of the Puritans. With respect to what is said of the necessity of protecting society from the bad example set to others by the vicious or the self-indulgent; it is true that bad example may have a pernicious effect, especially the example of doing wrong to others with impunity to the wrong-doer. But we are now speaking of conduct which, while it does no wrong to others, is supposed to do great harm to the agent himself; and I do not see how those who believe this, can think otherwise than that the example, on the whole, must be more salutary than hurtful, since, if it displays the misconduct, it displays also the painful or degrading consequences which, if the conduct is justly censured, must be supposed to be in all or most cases attendant on it.

But the strongest of all the arguments against the interference of the public with purely personal conduct, is that when it does interfere, the odds are that it interferes wrongly, and in the wrong place. On questions of social morality, of duty to others, the opinion of the public, that is, of an overruling majority, though often wrong, is likely to be still oftener right; because on such questions they are only required to judge of their own interests; of the manner in which some mode of conduct, if allowed to be practised, would affect themselves. But the opinion of a similar majority, imposed as a law on the minority, on questions of self-regarding conduct, is quite as likely to be wrong as right; for in these cases public opinion means, at the best, some people's opinion of what is good or bad for other people; while very often it does not even mean that; the public, with the most perfect indifference, passing over the pleasure or convenience of those whose conduct they censure, and considering only their own preference. There are many who consider as an injury to themselves any conduct which they have a distaste for, and resent it as an outrage to their feelings; as a religious bigot, when charged with disregarding the religious feelings of others, has been known to retort that they disregard his feelings, by persisting in their abominable worship or creed. But there is no parity between the feeling of a person for his own opinion, and the feeling of another who is offended at his holding it; no more than between the desire of a thief to take a purse, and the desire of the right owner to keep it. And a person's taste is as much his own peculiar concern as his opinion or his purse. It is easy for any one to imagine an ideal public, which leaves the freedom and choice of individuals in all uncertain matters undisturbed, and only requires them to abstain from modes of conduct which universal experience has condemned. But where has there been seen a public which set any such limit to its censorship? or when does the public trouble itself about universal experience? In its interferences with personal conduct it is seldom thinking of anything but the enormity of acting or feeling differently from itself; and this standard of judgment, thinly disguised, is held up to mankind as the dictate of religion and philosophy, by nine-tenths of all moralists and speculative writers. These teach that things are right because they are right; because we feel them to be so. They tell us to search in our own minds and hearts for laws of conduct binding on ourselves and on all others. What can the poor public do but apply these instructions, and make their own personal feelings of good and evil, if they are tolerably unanimous in them, obligatory on all the world?

The evil here pointed out is not one which exists only in theory; and it may perhaps be expected that I should specify the instances in which the public of this age and country improperly invests its own preferences with the character of moral laws. I am not writing an essay on the aberrations of existing moral feeling. That is too weighty a subject to be discussed parenthetically, and by way of illustration. Yet examples are necessary, to show that the principle I maintain is of serious and practical moment, and that I am not endeavouring to erect a barrier against imaginary evils. And it is not difficult to show, by abundant instances, that to extend the bounds of what may be called moral police, until it encroaches on the most unquestionably legitimate liberty of the individual, is one of the most universal of all human propensities.

As a first instance, consider the antipathies which men cherish on no better grounds than that persons whose religious opinions are different from theirs, do not practise their religious observances, especially their religious abstinences. To cite a rather trivial example, nothing in the creed or practice of Christians does more to envenom the hatred of Mahomedans against them, than the fact of their eating pork. There are few acts which Christians and Europeans regard with more unaffected disgust, than Mussulmans regard this particular mode of satisying hunger. It is, in the first place, an offence against their religion; but this circumstance by no means explains either the degree or the kind of their repugnance; for wine also is forbidden by their religion, and to partake of it is by all Mussulmans accounted wrong, but not disgusting. Their aversion to the flesh of the 'unclean beast' is, on the contrary, of that peculiar character, resembling an instinctive antipathy, which the idea of uncleanness, when once it thoroughly sinks into the feelings, seems always to excite even in those whose personal habits are anything but scrupulously clean, and of which the sentiment of religious impurity, so intense in the Hindoos, is a remarkable example. Suppose now that in a people, of whom the majority were Mussulmans, that majority should insist upon not permitting pork to be eaten within the limits of the country. This would be nothing new in Mahomedan countries.[1] Would it be a legitimate exercise of the moral authority of public opinion? and if not, why not? The practice is really revolting to such a public. They also sincerely think that it is forbidden and abhorred by the Deity. Neither could the prohibition be censured as religious persecution. It might be religious in its origin, but it would not be persecution for religion, since nobody's religion makes it a duty to eat pork. The only tenable ground of condemnation would be, that with the personal tastes and self-regarding concerns of individuals the public has no business to interfere. . . .

Under the name of preventing intemperance, the people of one English colony, and of nearly half the United States, have been interdicted by law from making any use whatever of fermented drinks, except for medical purposes: for prohibition of their sale is in fact, as it is intended to be, prohibition of their use. And though the impracticability of executing the law has caused its repeal in several of the States which had adopted it, including the one from which it derives its name, an attempt has notwithstanding been commenced, and is

---

[1] The case of the Bombay Parsees is a curious instance in point. When this industrious and enterprising tribe, the descendants of the Persian fire-worshippers, flying from their native country before the Caliphs, arrived in Western India, they were admitted to toleration by the Hindoo sovereigns, on condition of not eating beef. When those regions afterwards fell under the dominion of Mahomedan conquerors, the Parsees obtained from them a continuance of indulgence, on condition of refraining from pork. What was at first obedience to authority became a second nature, and the Parsees to this day abstain both from beef and pork. Though not required by their religion, the double abstinence has had time to grow into a custom of their tribe: and custom, in the East, is a religion.

prosecuted with considerable zeal by many of the professed philanthropists, to agitate for a similar law in this country. The association, or 'Alliance' as it terms itself, which has been formed for this purpose, has acquired some notoriety through the publicity given to a correspondence between its Secretary and one of the very few English public men who hold that a politician's opinions ought to be founded on principles. Lord Stanley's share in this correspondence is calculated to strengthen the hopes already built on him, by those who know how rare such qualities as are manifested in some of his public appearances, unhappily are among those who figure in political life. The organ of the Alliance, who would 'deeply deplore the recognition of any principle which could be wrested to justify bigotry and persecution,' undertakes to point out the 'broad and impassable barrier' which divides such principles from those of the association. 'All matters relating to thought, opinion, conscience, appear to me,' he says, 'to be without the sphere of legislation; all pertaining to social act, habit, relation, subject only to a discretionary power vested in the State itself, and not in the individual, to be within it.' No mention is made of a third class, different from either of these, viz. acts and habits which are not social, but individual; although it is to this class, surely, that the act of drinking fermented liquors belongs. Selling fermented liquors, however, is trading, and trading is a social act. But the infringement complained of is not on the liberty of the seller, but on that of the buyer and consumer; since the State might just as well forbid him to drink wine, as purposely make it impossible for him to obtain it. The Secretary, however, says, 'I claim, as a citizen, a right to legislate whenever my social rights are invaded by the social act of another.' And now for the definition of these 'social rights.' 'If anything invades my social rights, certainly the traffic in strong drink does. It destroys my primary right of security, by constantly creating and stimulating social disorder. It invades my right of equality, by deriving a profit from the creation of a misery, I am taxed to support. It impedes my right to free moral and intellectual development, by surrounding my path with dangers, and by weakening and demoralizing society, from which I have a right to claim mutual aid and intercourse.' A theory of 'social rights,' the like of which probably never before found its way into distinct language—being nothing short of this—that it is the absolute social right of every individual, that every other individual shall act in every respect exactly as he ought; that whosoever fails thereof in the smallest particular, violates my social right, and entitles me to demand from the legislature the removal of the grievance. So monstrous a principle is far more dangerous than any single interference with liberty; there is no violation of liberty which it would not justify; it acknowledges no right to any freedom whatever, except perhaps to that of holding opinions in secret, without ever disclosing them: for the moment an opinion which I consider noxious, passes any one's lips, it invades all the 'social rights' attributed to me by the Alliance. The doctrine ascribes to all mankind a vested interest in each other's moral, intellectual, and even physical perfection to be defined by each claimant according to his own standard. . . .

I cannot refrain from adding to these examples of the little account commonly made of human liberty, the language of downright persecution which breaks out from the press of this country, whenever it feels called on to notice the remarkable phenomenon of Mormonism. Much might be said on the unexpected and instructive fact, that an alleged new revelation, and a religion founded on it, the product of palpable imposture, not even supported by the *prestige* of extraordinary qualities in its founder, is believed by hundreds of thousands, and has been made the foundation of a society, in the age of newspapers, railways, and the electric telegraph. What here concerns us is, that this religion, like other and better religions, has its martyrs; that its prophet and founder was, for his teaching, put to death by a mob; that others of its adherents lost their lives by the same lawless violence; that they were forcibly expelled, in a body, from the country in which they first grew up; while, now that they have been chased into a solitary recess in the midst of a desert, many in this country openly declare that it would be right (only that it is not convenient) to send an expedition against them, and compel them by force to conform to the opinions of other people. The article of the Mormonite doctrine which is the chief provocative to the antipathy which thus breaks through the ordinary restraints of religious tolerance, is its sanction of polygamy; which, though permitted to Mahomedans, and Hindoos, and Chinese, seems to excite unquenchable animosity when practised by persons who speak English, and profess to be a kind of Christians. No one has a deeper disapprobation than I have of this Mormon institution; both for other reasons, and because, far from being in any way countenanced by the principle of liberty, it is a direct infraction of that principle, being a mere riveting of the chains of one half of the community, and an emancipation of the other from reciprocity of obligation towards them. Still, it must be remembered that this relation is as much voluntary on the part of the women concerned in it, and who may be deemed the sufferers by it, as is the case with any other form of the marriage institution; and however surprising this fact may appear, it has its explanation in the common ideas and customs of the world, which, teaching women to think marriage the one thing needful, make it intelligible that many a woman should prefer being one of several wives, to not being a wife at all. Other countries are not asked to recognise such unions, or release any portion of their inhabitants from their own laws on the score of Mormonite opinions. But when the dissentients have conceded to the hostile sentiments of others, far more than could justly be demanded; when they have left the countries to which their doctrines were unacceptable, and established themselves in a remote corner of the earth, which they have been the first to render habitable to human beings; it is difficult to see on what principles but those of tyranny they can be prevented from living there under what laws they please, provided they commit no aggression on other nations, and allow perfect freedom of departure to those who are dissatisfied with their ways. A recent writer, in some respects of considerable merit, proposes (to use his own words), not a crusade, but a *civilizade,* against this polygamous community, to put an end to what seems to him a retrograde step in civilization. It also appears so to me, but I am not aware that any community has a right to force another to be civilized. So long as the sufferers by the bad law do not invoke assistance from other communities, I cannot admit that persons entirely unconnected with them ought to step in and require that a condition of things with which all who are directly interested appear to be satisfied, should be put an end to because it is a scandal to persons some thousands of miles distant, who have no part or concern in it. Let them send missionaries, if they please, to preach against it; and let them, by any fair means (of which silencing the teachers is not one) oppose the progress of similar doctrines among their own people. If civilization has got the better of barbarism when barbarism had the world to itself, it is too much to profess to be afraid lest barbarism, after having been fairly got under, should revive and conquer civilization. A civilization that can thus succumb to its vanquished enemy, must first have become so degenerate, that neither its appointed priests and teachers, nor any body else, has the capacity, or will take the trouble, to stand up for it. If this be so, the sooner such a civilization receives notice to quit, the better. It can only go on from bad to worse, until destroyed and regenerated (like the Western Empire) by energetic barbarians.

Lord Patrick Devlin

Morals and the
Criminal Law

24 The Report of the Committee on Homosexual Offences and
Prostitution, generally known as the Wolfenden Report, is
recognized to be an excellent study of two very difficult legal
and social problems. But it has also a particular claim to the
respect of those interested in jurisprudence; it does what law
reformers so rarely do; it sets out clearly and carefully what
in relation to its subjects it considers the function of the law
to be.[1] Statutory additions to the criminal law are too often
made on the simple principle that 'there ought to be a law
against it'. The greater part of the law relating to sexual offences is the creation of statute and it is difficult to ascertain
any logical relationship between it and the moral ideas which
most of us uphold. Adultery, fornication, and prostitution are
not, as the Report[2] points out, criminal offences: homosexuality between males is a criminal offence, but between females
it is not. Incest was not an offence until it was declared so by
statute only fifty years ago. Does the legislature select
these offences haphazardly or are there some principles which
can be used to determine what part of the moral law should

Lord Patrick Devlin was born in 1905 and served as Justice of the High
Court, Queens Bench, from 1948–1960, and as Lord of Appeal from 1961–
1964. He is the author of *Trial by Jury* (1956), *The Criminal Prosecution in
England* (1957), and *Samples of Lawmaking* (1962).
This essay "Morals and the Criminal Law" is based upon the Maccabaean
lecture in jurisprudence, 1959, of the British Academy, entitled "The Enforcement of Morals." The lecture was published under the same title in
1959. It was reprinted, with some changes, under its present title in 1965,
in a collection of essays by Lord Devlin entitled *The Enforcement of Morals.*
The essay is reprinted here with the permission of Lord Devlin and the
Oxford University Press.

[1] The Committee's 'statement of juristic philosophy' (to quote Lord Paken-
ham) was considered by him in a debate in the House of Lords on 4
December 1957, reported in *Hansard Lords Debates,* vol. ccvi at 738; and
also in the same debate by the Archbishop of Canterbury at 753 and Lord
Denning at 806. The subject has also been considered by Mr. J. E. Hall
Williams in the *Law Quarterly Review,* January 1958, vol. lxxiv, p. 76.

[2] Para. 14.

be embodied in the criminal? There is, for example, being now considered a proposal to make A.I.D., that is, the practice of artificial insemination of a woman with the seed of a man who is not her husband, a criminal offence; if, as is usually the case, the woman is married, this is in substance, if not in form, adultery. Ought it to be made punishable when adultery is not? This sort of question is of practical importance, for a law that appears to be arbitrary and illogical, in the end and after the wave of moral indignation that has put it on the statute book subsides, forfeits respect. As a practical question it arises more frequently in the field of sexual morals than in any other, but there is no special answer to be found in that field. The inquiry must be general and fundamental. What is the connexion between crime and sin and to what extent, if at all, should the criminal law of England concern itself with the enforcement of morals and punish sin or immorality as such?

The statements of principle in the Wolfenden Report provide an admirable and modern starting-point for such an inquiry. In the course of my examination of them I shall find matter for criticism. If my criticisms are sound, it must not be imagined that they point to any shortcomings in the Report. Its authors were not, as I am trying to do, composing a paper on the jurisprudence of morality; they were evolving a working formula to use for reaching a number of practical conclusions. I do not intend to express any opinion one way or the other about these; that would be outside the scope of a lecture on jurisprudence. I am concerned only with general principles; the statement of these in the Report illuminates the entry into the subject and I hope that its authors will forgive me if I carry the lamp with me into places where it was not intended to go.

Early in the Report[3] the Committee put forward:

Our own formulation of the function of the criminal law so far as it concerns the subjects of this enquiry. In this field, its function, as we see it, is to preserve public order and decency, to protect the citizen from what is offensive or injurious, and to provide sufficient safeguards against exploitation and corruption of others, particularly those who are specially vulnerable because they are young, weak in body or mind, inexperienced, or in a state of special physical, official or economic dependence.

[3] Para. 13.

It is not, in our view, the function of the law to intervene in the private lives of citizens, or to seek to enforce any particular pattern of behaviour, further than is necessary to carry out the purposes we have outlined.

The Committee preface their most important recommendation[4]

that homosexual behaviour between consenting adults in private should no longer be a criminal offence, [by stating the argument[5]] which we believe to be decisive, namely, the importance which society and the law ought to give to individual freedom of choice and action in matters of private morality. Unless a deliberate attempt is to be made by society, acting through the agency of the law, to equate the sphere of crime with that of sin, there must remain a realm of private morality and immorality which is, in brief and crude terms, not the law's business. To say this is not to condone or encourage private immorality.

Similar statements of principle are set out in the chapters of the Report which deal with prostitution. No case can be sustained, the Report says, for attempting to make prostitution itself illegal.[6] The Committee refer to the general reasons already given and add: 'We are agreed that private immorality should not be the concern of the criminal law except in the special circumstances therein mentioned.' They quote[7] with approval the report of the Street Offences Committee,[8] which says: 'As a general proposition it will be universally accepted that the law is not concerned with private morals or with ethical sanctions.' It will be observed that the emphasis is on *private* immorality. By this is meant immorality which is not offensive or injurious to the public in the ways defined or described in the first passage which I quoted. In other words, no act of immorality should be made a criminal offence unless it is accompanied by some other feature such as indecency, corruption, or exploitation. This is clearly brought out in relation to prostitution: 'It is not the duty of the law to concern

[4] Para. 62.
[5] Para. 61.
[6] Para. 224.
[7] Para. 227.
[8] Cmd. 3231 (1928).

itself with immorality as such . . . it should confine itself to those activities which offend against public order and decency or expose the ordinary citizen to what is offensive or injurious.'[9]

These statements of principle are naturally restricted to the subject-matter of the Report. But they are made in general terms and there seems to be no reason why, if they are valid, they should not be applied to the criminal law in general. They separate very decisively crime from sin, the divine law from the secular, and the moral from the criminal. They do not signify any lack of support for the law, moral or criminal, and they do not represent an attitude that can be called either religious or irreligious. There are many schools of thought among those who may think that morals are not the law's business. There is first of all the agnostic or free-thinker. He does not of course disbelieve in morals, nor in sin if it be given the wider of the two meanings assigned to it in the *Oxford English Dictionary* where it is defined as 'transgression against divine law or the principles of morality.' He cannot accept the divine law; that does not mean that he might not view with suspicion any departure from moral principles that have for generations been accepted by the society in which he lives; but in the end he judges for himself. Then there is the deeply religious person who feels that the criminal law is sometimes more of a hindrance than a help in the sphere of morality, and that the reform of the sinner—at any rate when he injures only himself—should be a spiritual rather than a temporal work. Then there is the man who without any strong feeling cannot see why, where there is freedom in religious belief, there should not logically be freedom in morality as well. All these are powerfully allied against the equating of crime with sin.

I must disclose at the outset that I have as a judge an interest in the result of the inquiry which I am seeking to make as a jurisprudent. As a judge who administers the criminal law and who has often to pass sentence in a criminal court, I should feel handicapped in my task if I thought that I was addressing an audience which had no sense of sin or which thought of crime as something quite different. Ought one, for example, in passing sentence upon a female abortionist to treat her simply as if she were an unlicensed midwife? If not, why not? But if so, is all the panoply of the law erected over a set of social regulations? I must admit that I begin with a feel-

[9] Para. 257.

ing that a complete separation of crime from sin (I use the term throughout this lecture in the wider meaning) would not be good for the moral law and might be disastrous for the criminal. But can this sort of feeling be justified as a matter of jurisprudence? And if it be a right feeling, how should the relationship between the criminal and the moral law be stated? Is there a good theoretical basis for it, or is it just a practical working alliance, or is it a bit of both? That is the problem which I want to examine, and I shall begin by considering the standpoint of the strict logician. It can be supported by cogent arguments, some of which I believe to be unanswerable and which I put as follows.

Morals and religion are inextricably joined—the moral standards generally accepted in Western civilization being those belonging to Christianity. Outside Christendom other standards derive from other religions. None of these moral codes can claim any validity except by virtue of the religion on which it is based. Old Testament morals differ in some respects from New Testament morals. Even within Christianity there are differences. Some hold that contraception is an immoral practice and that a man who has carnal knowledge of another woman while his wife is alive is in all circumstances a fornicator; others, including most of the English-speaking world, deny both these propositions. Between the great religions of the world, of which Christianity is only one, there are much wider differences. It may or may not be right for the State to adopt one of these religions as the truth, to found itself upon its doctrines, and to deny to any of its citizens the liberty to practise any other. If it does, it is logical that it should use the secular law wherever it thinks it necessary to enforce the divine. If it does not, it is illogical that it should concern itself with morals as such. But if it leaves matters of religion to private judgement, it should logically leave matters of morals also. A State which refuses to enforce Christian beliefs has lost the right to enforce Christian morals.

If this view is sound, it means that the criminal law cannot justify any of its provisions by reference to the moral law. It cannot say, for example, that murder and theft are prohibited because they are immoral or sinful. The State must justify in some other way the punishments which it imposes on wrongdoers and a function for the criminal law independent of morals must be found. This is not difficult to do. The smooth functioning of society and the preservation of order require that a number of activities should be regulated. The rules that are made for that purpose and are enforced by the criminal

law are often designed simply to achieve uniformity and convenience and rarely involve any choice between good and
evil. Rules that impose a speed limit or prevent obstruction on
the highway have nothing to do with morals. Since so much of
the criminal law is composed of rules of this sort, why bring
morals into it at all? Why not define the function of the criminal
law in simple terms as the preservation of order and decency
and the protection of the lives and property of citizens, and
elaborate those terms in relation to any particular subject in
the way in which it is done in the Wolfenden Report? The
criminal law in carrying out these objects will undoubtedly
overlap the moral law. Crimes of violence are morally wrong
and they are also offences against good order; therefore they
offend against both laws. But this is simply because the two
laws in pursuit of different objectives happen to cover the
same area. Such is the argument.

Is the argument consistent or inconsistent with the fundamental principles of English criminal law as it exists today?
That is the first way of testing it, though by no means a con-
clusive one. In the field of jurisprudence one is at liberty to
overturn even fundamental conceptions if they are theoretically unsound. But to see how the argument fares under the
existing law is a good starting-point.

It is true that for many centuries the criminal law was much
concerned with keeping the peace and little, if at all, with
sexual morals. But it would be wrong to infer from that that it
had no moral content or that it would ever have tolerated the
idea of a man being left to judge for himself in matters of
morals. The criminal law of England has from the very first
concerned itself with moral principles. A simple way of testing
this point is to consider the attitude which the criminal law
adopts towards consent.

Subject to certain exceptions inherent in the nature of particular crimes, the criminal law has never permitted consent
of the victim to be used as a defence. In rape, for example,
consent negatives an essential element. But consent of the
victim is no defence to a charge of murder. It is not a defence
to any form of assault that the victim thought his punishment
well deserved and submitted to it; to make a good defence the
accused must prove that the law gave him the right to chastise
and that he exercised it reasonably. Likewise, the victim may
not forgive the aggressor and require the prosecution to de-
sist; the right to enter a *nolle prosequi* belongs to the Attorney-
General alone.

Now, if the law existed for the protection of the individual, there would be no reason why he should avail himself of it if he did not want it. The reason why a man may not consent to the commission of an offence against himself beforehand or forgive it afterwards is because it is an offence against society. It is not that society is physically injured; that would be impossible. Nor need any individual be shocked, corrupted, or exploited; everything may be done in private. Nor can it be explained on the practical ground that a violent man is a potential danger to others in the community who have therefore a direct interest in his apprehension and punishment as being necessary to their own protection. That would be true of a man whom the victim is prepared to forgive but not of one who gets his consent first; a murderer who acts only upon the consent, and maybe the request, of his victim is no menace to others, but he does threaten one of the great moral principles upon which society is based, that is, the sanctity of human life. There is only one explanation of what has hitherto been accepted as the basis of the criminal law and that is that there are certain standards of behaviour or moral principles which society requires to be observed; and the breach of them is an offence not merely against the person who is injured but against society as a whole.

Thus, if the criminal law were to be reformed so as to eliminate from it everything that was not designed to preserve order and decency or to protect citizens (including the protection of youth from corruption), it would overturn a fundamental principle. It would also end a number of specific crimes. Euthanasia or the killing of another at his own request, suicide, attempted suicide and suicide pacts, duelling, abortion, incest between brother and sister, are all acts which can be done in private and without offence to others and need not involve the corruption or exploitation of others. Many people think that the law on some of these subjects is in need of reform, but no one hitherto has gone so far as to suggest that they should all be left outside the criminal law as matters of private morality. They can be brought within it only as a matter of moral principle. It must be remembered also that although there is much immorality that is not punished by the law, there is none that is condoned by the law. The law will not allow its processes to be used by those engaged in immorality of any sort. For example, a house may not be let for immoral purposes; the lease is invalid and would not be enforced. But if what goes on inside there is a matter of private morality and not the law's business, why does the law inquire into it at all?

I think it is clear that the criminal law as we know it is based upon moral principle. In a number of crimes its function is simply to enforce a moral principle and nothing else. The law, both criminal and civil, claims to be able to speak about morality and immorality generally. Where does it get its authority to do this and how does it settle the moral principles which it enforces? Undoubtedly, as a matter of history, it derived both from Christian teaching. But I think that the strict logician is right when he says that the law can no longer rely on doctrines in which citizens are entitled to disbelieve. It is necessary therefore to look for some other source.

In jurisprudence, as I have said, everything is thrown open to discussion and, in the belief that they cover the whole field, I have framed three interrogatories addressed to myself to answer:

1. Has society the right to pass judgement at all on matters of morals? Ought there, in other words, to be a public morality, or are morals always a matter for private judgement?

2. If society has the right to pass judgement, has it also the right to use the weapon of the law to enforce it?

3. If so, ought it to use that weapon in all cases or only in some; and if only in some, on what principles should it distinguish?

I shall begin with the first interrogatory and consider what is meant by the right of society to pass a moral judgement, that is, a judgement about what is good and what is evil. The fact that a majority of people may disapprove of a practice does not of itself make it a matter for society as a whole. Nine men out of ten may disapprove of what the tenth man is doing and still say that it is not their business. There is a case for a collective judgement (as distinct from a large number of individual opinions which sensible people may even refrain from pronouncing at all if it is upon somebody else's private affairs) only if society is affected. Without a collective judgement there can be no case at all for intervention. Let me take as an illustration the Englishman's attitude to religion as it is now and as it has been in the past. His attitude now is that a man's religion is his private affair; he may think of another man's religion that it is right or wrong, true or untrue, but not that it is good or bad. In earlier times that was not so; a man was denied the right to practise what was thought of as heresy, and heresy was thought of as destructive of society.

The language used in the passages I have quoted from the Wolfenden Report suggests the view that there ought not to be a collective judgement about immorality *per se*. Is this what is meant by 'private morality' and 'individual freedom of choice and action'? Some people sincerely believe that homosexuality is neither immoral nor unnatural. Is the 'freedom of choice and action' that is offered to the individual, freedom to decide for himself what is moral or immoral, society remaining neutral; or is it freedom to be immoral if he wants to be? The language of the Report may be open to question, but the conclusions at which the Committee arrive answer this question unambiguously. If society is not prepared to say that homosexuality is morally wrong, there would be no basis for a law protecting youth from 'corruption' or punishing a man for living on the 'immoral' earnings of a homosexual prostitute, as the Report recommends.[10] This attitude the Committee make even clearer when they come to deal with prostitution. In truth, the Report takes it for granted that there is in existence a public morality which condemns homosexuality and prostitution. What the Report seems to mean by private morality might perhaps be better described as private behaviour in matters of morals.

This view—that there is such a thing as public morality— can also be justified by *a priori* argument. What makes a society of any sort is community of ideas, not only political ideas but also ideas about the way its members should behave and govern their lives; these latter ideas are its morals. Every society has a moral structure as well as a political one: or rather, since that might suggest two independent systems, I should say that the structure of every society is made up both of politics and morals. Take, for example, the institution of marriage. Whether a man should be allowed to take more than one wife is something about which every society has to make up its mind one way or the other. In England we believe in the Christian idea of marriage and therefore adopt monogamy as a moral principle. Consequently the Christian institution of marriage has become the basis of family life and so part of the structure of our society. It is there not because it is Christian. It has got there because it is Christian, but it remains there because it is built into the house in which we live and could not be removed without bringing it down. The great majority of those who live in this country accept it because it is the Christian idea of marriage and for them the only true one. But a non-Christian is bound by it, not because it is part of Christianity but because, rightly or wrongly, it has been adopted by

---

[10] Para. 76.

the society in which he lives. It would be useless for him to stage a debate designed to prove that polygamy was theologically more correct and socially preferable; if he wants to live in the house, he must accept it as built in the way in which it is.

We see this more clearly if we think of ideas or institutions that are purely political. Society cannot tolerate rebellion; it will not allow argument about the rightness of the cause. Historians a century later may say that the rebels were right and the Government was wrong and a percipient and conscientious subject of the State may think so at the time. But it is not a matter which can be left to individual judgement.

The institution of marriage is a good example for my purpose because it bridges the division, if there is one, between politics and morals. Marriage is part of the structure of our society and it is also the basis of a moral code which condemns fornication and adultery. The institution of marriage would be gravely threatened if individual judgements were permitted about the morality of adultery; on these points there must be a public morality. But public morality is not to be confined to those moral principles which support institutions such as marriage. People do not think of monogamy as something which has to be supported because our society has chosen to organize itself upon it; they think of it as something that is good in itself and offering a good way of life and that it is for that reason that our society has adopted it. I return to the statement that I have already made, that society means a community of ideas; without shared ideas on politics, morals, and ethics no society can exist. Each one of us has ideas about what is good and what is evil; they cannot be kept private from the society in which we live. If men and women try to create a society in which there is no fundamental agreement about good and evil they will fail; if, having based it on common agreement, the agreement goes, the society will disintegrate. For society is not something that is kept together physically; it is held by the invisible bonds of common thought. If the bonds were too far relaxed the members would drift apart. A common morality is part of the bondage. The bondage is part of the price of society; and mankind, which needs society, must pay its price.

Common lawyers used to say that Christianity was part of the law of the land. That was never more than a piece of rhetoric as Lord Sumner said in *Bowman* v. *The Secular Society*.[11] What lay behind it was the notion which I have been

[11] (1917), A.C. 406, at 457.

seeking to expound, namely that morals—and up till a century or so ago no one thought it worth distinguishing between religion and morals—were necessary to the temporal order. In 1675 Chief Justice Hale said: 'To say that religion is a cheat is to dissolve all those obligations whereby civil society is preserved.'[12] In 1797 Mr. Justice Ashurst said of blasphemy that it was 'not only an offence against God but against all law and government from its tendency to dissolve all the bonds and obligations of civil society.'[13] By 1908 Mr. Justice Phillimore was able to say: 'A man is free to think, to speak and to teach what he pleases as to religious matters, but not as to morals.'[14]

You may think that I have taken far too long in contending that there is such a thing as public morality, a proposition which most people would readily accept, and may have left myself too little time to discuss the next question which to many minds may cause greater difficulty: to what extent should society use the law to enforce its moral judgements? But I believe that the answer to the first question determines the way in which the second should be approached and may indeed very nearly dictate the answer to the second question. If society has no right to make judgements on morals, the law must find some special justification for entering the field of morality: if homosexuality and prostitution are not in themselves wrong, then the onus is very clearly on the lawgiver who wants to frame a law against certain aspects of them to justify the exceptional treatment. But if society has the right to make a judgement and has it on the basis that a recognized morality is as necessary to society as, say, a recognized government, then society may use the law to preserve morality in the same way as it uses it to safeguard anything else that is essential to its existence. If therefore the first proposition is securely established with all its implications, society has a prima facie right to legislate against immorality as such.

The Wolfenden Report, notwithstanding that it seems to admit the right of society to condemn homosexuality and prostitution as immoral, requires special circumstances to be shown to justify the intervention of the law. I think that this is wrong in principle and that any attempt to approach my second interrogatory on these lines is bound to break down. I think that the attempt by the Committee does break down and

---

12 *Taylor's Case*, 1 Vent. 293.
13 *R.* v. *Williams*, 26 St. Tr. 653, at 715.
14 *R.* v. *Boulter*, 72 J.P. 188.

that this is shown by the fact that it has to define or describe its special circumstances so widely that they can be supported only if it is accepted that the law *is* concerned with immorality as such.

The widest of the special circumstances are described as the provision of 'sufficient safeguards against exploitation and corruption of others, particularly those who are specially vulnerable because they are young, weak in body or mind, inexperienced, or in a state of special physical, official or economic dependence.'[15] The corruption of youth is a well-recognized ground for intervention by the State and for the purpose of any legislation the young can easily be defined. But if similar protection were to be extended to every other citizen, there would be no limit to the reach of the law. The 'corruption and exploitation of others' is so wide that it could be used to cover any sort of immorality which involves, as most do, the co-operation of another person. Even if the phrase is taken as limited to the categories that are particularized as 'specially vulnerable', it is so elastic as to be practically no restriction. This is not merely a matter of words. For if the words used are stretched almost beyond breaking-point, they still are not wide enough to cover the recommendations which the Committee make about prostitution.

Prostitution is not in itself illegal and the Committee do not think that it ought to be made so.[16] If prostitution is private immorality and not the law's business, what concern has the law with the ponce or the brothel-keeper or the householder who permits habitual prostitution? The Report recommends that the laws which make these activities criminal offences should be maintained or strengthened and brings them (so far as it goes into principle; with regard to brothels it says simply that the law rightly frowns on them) under the head of exploitation.[17] There may be cases of exploitation in this trade, as there are or used to be in many others, but in general a ponce exploits a prostitute no more than an impresario exploits an actress. The Report finds that 'the great majority of prostitutes are women whose psychological makeup is such that they choose this life because they find in it a style of living which is to them easier, freer and more profitable than would be provided by any other occupation. . . . In the main the association between prostitute and ponce is voluntary and operates to

15 Para. 13.
16 Paras. 224, 285, and 318.
17 Paras. 302 and 320.

mutual advantage.'[18] The Committee would agree that this could not be called exploitation in the ordinary sense. They say: 'It is in our view an over-simplification to think that those who live on the earnings of prostitution are exploiting the prostitute as such. What they are really exploiting is the whole complex of the relationship between prostitute and customer; they are, in effect, exploiting the human weaknesses which cause the customer to seek the prostitute and the prostitute to meet the demand.'[19]

All sexual immorality involves the exploitation of human weaknesses. The prostitute exploits the lust of her customers and the customer the moral weakness of the prostitute. If the exploitation of human weaknesses is considered to create a special circumstance, there is virtually no field of morality which can be defined in such a way as to exclude the law.

I think, therefore, that it is not possible to set theoretical limits to the power of the State to legislate against immorality. It is not possible to settle in advance exceptions to the general rule or to define inflexibly areas of morality into which the law is in no circumstances to be allowed to enter. Society is entitled by means of its laws to protect itself from dangers, whether from within or without. Here again I think that the political parallel is legitimate. The law of treason is directed against aiding the king's enemies and against sedition from within. The justification for this is that established government is necessary for the existence of society and therefore its safety against violent overthrow must be secured. But an established morality is as necessary as good government to the welfare of society. Societies disintegrate from within more frequently than they are broken up by external pressures. There is disintegration when no common morality is observed and history shows that the loosening of moral bonds is often the first stage of disintegration, so that society is justified in taking the same steps to preserve its moral code as it does to preserve its government and other essential institutions.[20] The

---

[18] Para. 223.

[19] Para. 306.

[20] It is somewhere about this point in the argument that Professor Hart in *Law, Liberty and Morality* discerns a proposition which he describes as central to my thought. He states the proposition and his objection to it as follows (p. 51). 'He appears to move from the acceptable proposition that *some* shared morality is essential to the existence of any society [this I take to be the proposition on p. 12] to the unacceptable proposition that a society is identical with its morality as that is at any given moment of its history so that a change in its morality is tantamount to the destruction of a society. The former proposition might be even accepted as a necessary rather than an empirical truth depending on a quite plausible definition of

suppression of vice is as much the law's business as the suppression of subversive activities; it is no more possible to define a sphere of private morality than it is to define one of private subversive activity. It is wrong to talk of private morality or of the law not being concerned with immorality as such or to try to set rigid bounds to the part which the law may play in the suppression of vice. There are no theoretical limits to the power of the State to legislate against treason and sedition, and likewise I think there can be no theoretical limits to legislation against immorality. You may argue that if a man's sins affect only himself it cannot be the concern of society. If he chooses to get drunk every night in the privacy of his own home, is any one except himself the worse for it? But suppose a quarter or a half of the population got drunk every night, what sort of society would it be? You cannot set a theoretical limit to the number of people who can get drunk before society is entitled to legislate against drunkenness. The same

---

society as a body of men who hold certain moral views in common. But the latter proposition is absurd. Taken strictly, it would prevent us saying that the morality of a given society had changed, and would compel us instead to say that one society had disappeared and another one taken its place. But it is only on this absurd criterion of what it is for the same society to continue to exist that it could be asserted without evidence that any deviation from a society's shared morality threatens its existence.' In conclusion (p. 82) Professor Hart condemns the whole thesis in the lecture as based on 'a confused definition of what a society is.'

I do not assert that *any* deviation from a society's shared morality threatens its existence any more than I assert that *any* subversive activity threatens its existence. I assert that they are both activities which are capable in their nature of threatening the existence of society so that neither can be put beyond the law.

For the rest, the objection appears to me to be all a matter of words. I would venture to assert, for example, that you cannot have a game without rules and that if there were no rules there would be no game. If I am asked whether that means that the game is 'identical' with the rules, I would be willing for the question to be answered either way in the belief that the answer would lead to nowhere. If I am asked whether a change in the rules means that one game has disappeared and another has taken its place, I would reply probably not, but that it would depend on the extent of the change.

Likewise I should venture to assert that there cannot be a contract without terms. Does this mean that an 'amended' contract is a 'new' contract in the eyes of the law? I once listened to an argument by an ingenious counsel that a contract, because of the substitution of one clause for another, had 'ceased to have effect' within the meaning of a statutory provision. The judge did not accept the argument; but if most of the fundamental terms had been changed, I daresay he would have done.

The proposition that I make in the text is that if (as I understand Professor Hart to agree, at any rate for the purposes of the argument) you cannot have a society without morality, the law can be used to enforce morality as something that is essential to a society. I cannot see why this proposition (whether it is right or wrong) should mean that morality can never be changed without the destruction of society. If morality is changed, the law can be changed. Professor Hart refers (p. 72) to the proposition as 'the use of legal punishment to freeze into immobility the morality dominant at a particular time in a society's existence.' One might as well say that the inclusion of a penal section into a statute prohibiting certain acts freezes the whole statute into immobility and prevents the prohibitions from ever being modified.

may be said of gambling. The Royal Commission on Betting, Lotteries, and Gaming took as their test the character of the citizen as a member of society. They said: 'Our concern with the ethical significance of gambling is confined to the effect which it may have on the character of the gambler as a member of society. If we were convinced that whatever the degree of gambling this effect must be harmful we should be inclined to think that it was the duty of the state to restrict gambling to the greatest extent practicable.'[21]

In what circumstances the State should exercise its power is the third of the interrogatories I have framed. But before I get to it I must raise a point which might have been brought up in any one of the three. How are the moral judgements of society to be ascertained? By leaving it until now, I can ask it in the more limited form that is now sufficient for my purpose. How is the law-maker to ascertain the moral judgements of society? It is surely not enough that they should be reached by the opinion of the majority; it would be too much to require the individual assent of every citizen. English law has evolved and regularly uses a standard which does not depend on the counting of heads. It is that of the reasonable man. He is not to be confused with the rational man. He is not expected to reason about anything and his judgement may be largely a matter of feeling. It is the viewpoint of the man in the street— or to use an archaism familiar to all lawyers—the man in the Clapham omnibus. He might also be called the right-minded man. For my purpose I should like to call him the man in the jury box, for the moral judgement of society must be something about which any twelve men or women drawn at random might after discussion be expected to be unanimous. This was the standard the judges applied in the days before Parliament was as active as it is now and when they laid down rules of public policy. They did not think of themselves as making law but simply as stating principles which every right-minded person would accept as valid. It is what Pollock called 'practical morality', which is based not on theological or philosophical foundations but 'in the mass of continuous experience half-consciously or unconsciously accumulated and embodied in the morality of common sense.' He called it also 'a certain way of thinking on question of morality which we expect to find in a reasonable civilized man or a reasonable Englishman, taken at random.'[22]

---

[21] (1951) Cmd. 8190, para. 159.
[22] *Essays in Jurisprudence and Ethics* (1882), Macmillan, pp. 278 and 353.

Immorality then, for the purpose of the law, is what every right-minded person is presumed to consider to be immoral. Any immorality is capable of affecting society injuriously and in effect to a greater or lesser extent it usually does; this is what gives the law its *locus standi.* It cannot be shut out. But —and this brings me to the third question—the individual has a *locus standi* too; he cannot be expected to surrender to the judgement of society the whole conduct of his life. It is the old and familiar question of striking a balance between the rights and interests of society and those of the individual. This is something which the law is constantly doing in matters large and small. To take a very down-to-earth example, let me consider the right of the individual whose house adjoins the highway to have access to it; that means in these days the right to have vehicles stationary in the highway, sometimes for a considerable time if there is a lot of loading or unloading. There are many cases in which the courts have had to balance the private right of access against the public right to use the highway without obstruction. It cannot be done by carving up the highway into public and private areas. It is done by recognizing that each have rights over the whole; that if each were to exercise their rights to the full, they would come into conflict; and therefore that the rights of each must be curtailed so as to ensure as far as possible that the essential needs of each are safeguarded.

I do not think that one can talk sensibly of a public and private morality any more than one can of a public or private highway. Morality is a sphere in which there is a public interest and a private interest, often in conflict, and the problem is to reconcile the two. This does not mean that it is impossible to put forward any general statements about how in our society the balance ought to be struck. Such statements cannot of their nature be rigid or precise; they would not be designed to circumscribe the operation of the law-making power but to guide those who have to apply it. While every decision which a court of law makes when it balances the public against the private interest is an *ad hoc* decision, the cases contain statements of principle to which the court should have regard when it reaches its decision. In the same way it is possible to make general statements of principle which it may be thought the legislature should bear in mind when it is considering the enactment of laws enforcing morals.

I believe that most people would agree upon the chief of these elastic principles. There must be toleration of the maximum individual freedom that is consistent with the integrity of society. It cannot be said that this is a principle that runs all through the criminal law. Much of the criminal law that is regulatory in character—the part of it that deals with *malum prohibitum* rather than *malum in se*—is based upon the opposite principle, that is, that the choice of the individual must give way to the convenience of the many. But in all matters of conscience the principle I have stated is generally held to prevail. It is not confined to thought and speech; it extends to action, as is shown by the recognition of the right to conscientious objection in war-time; this example shows also that conscience will be respected even in times of national danger. The principle appears to me to be peculiarly appropriate to all questions of morals. Nothing should be punished by the law that does not lie beyond the limits of tolerance. It is not nearly enough to say that a majority dislike a practice; there must be a real feeling of reprobation. Those who are dissatisfied with the present law on homosexuality often say that the opponents of reform are swayed simply by disgust. If that were so it would be wrong, but I do not think one can ignore disgust if it is deeply felt and not manufactured. Its presence is a good indication that the bounds of toleration are being reached. Not everything is to be tolerated. No society can do without intolerance, indignation, and disgust; they are the forces behind the moral law, and indeed it can be argued that if they or something like them are not present, the feelings of society cannot be weighty enough to deprive the individual of freedom of choice. I suppose that there is hardly anyone nowadays who would not be disgusted by the thought of deliberate cruelty to animals. No one proposes to relegate that or any other form of sadism to the realm of private morality or to allow it to be practised in public or in private. It would be possible no doubt to point out that until a comparatively short while ago nobody thought very much of cruelty to animals and also that pity and kindliness and the unwillingness to inflict pain are virtues more generally esteemed now than they have ever been in the past. But matters of this sort are not determined by rational argument. Every moral judgement, unless it claims a divine source, is simply a feeling that no right-minded man could behave in any other way without admitting that he was doing wrong. It is the power of a common sense and not the power of reason that is behind the judgements of society. But before a society can put a practice beyond the limits of tolerance there must be a deliberate judgement that the practice is injurious to society. There is, for example, a general abhorrence of homosexuality. We should ask ourselves in the first instance whether, looking at it calmly and dispassionately, we regard it as a vice so abominable that its mere presence is an offence. If that is the genuine feeling of the society in which we live, I do not see how society can be denied the right to eradicate it. Our feeling may not be so intense as that. We may feel about it that, if confined, it is tolerable, but that if it spread it might be gravely injurious; it is in this way that most societies look upon fornication, seeing it as a natural weakness which must be kept within bounds but which cannot be rooted out. It becomes then a question of balance, the danger to society in one scale and the extent of the restriction in the other. On this sort of point the value of an investigation by such a body as the Wolfenden Committee and of its conclusions is manifest.

The limits of tolerance shift. This is supplementary to what I have been saying but of sufficient importance in itself to deserve statement as a separate principle which law-makers have to bear in mind. I suppose that moral standards do not shift; so far as they come from divine revelation they do not, and I am willing to assume that the moral judgements made by a society always remain good for that society. But the extent to which society will tolerate—I mean tolerate, not approve—departures from moral standards varies from generation to generation. It may be that over-all tolerance is always increasing. The pressure of the human mind, always seeking greater freedom of thought, is outwards against the bonds of society forcing their gradual relaxation. It may be that history is a tale of contraction and expansion and that all developed societies are on their way to dissolution. I must not speak of things I do not know; and anyway as a practical matter no society is willing to make provision for its own decay. I return therefore to the simple and observable fact that in matters of morals the limits of tolerance shift. Laws, especially those which are based on morals, are less easily moved. It follows as another good working principle that in any new matter of morals the law should be slow to act. By the next generation the swell of indignation may have abated and the law be left without the strong backing which it needs. But it is then difficult to alter the law without giving the impression that moral judgement is being weakened. This is now one of the factors that is strongly militating against any alteration to the law on homosexuality.

A third elastic principle must be advanced more tentatively. It is that as far as possible privacy should be respected. This is not an idea that has ever been made explicit in the criminal law. Acts or words done or said in public or in private are all brought within its scope without distinction in principle. But there goes with this a strong reluctance on the part of judges and legislators to sanction invasions of privacy in the detection of crime. The police have no more right to trespass than the ordinary citizen has; there is no general right of search; to this extent an Englishman's home is still his castle. The Government is extremely careful in the exercise even of those powers which it claims to be undisputed. Telephone tapping and interference with the mails afford a good illustration of this. A Committee of three Privy Councillors who recently inquired[23] into these activities found that the Home Secretary and his predecessors had already formulated strict rules governing the exercise of these powers and the Committee were able to recommend that they should be continued to be exercised substantially on the same terms. But they reported that the power was 'regarded with general disfavour.'

This indicates a general sentiment that the right to privacy is something to be put in the balance against the enforcement of the law. Ought the same sort of consideration to play any part in the formation of the law? Clearly only in a very limited number of cases. When the help of the law is invoked by an injured citizen, privacy must be irrelevant; the individual cannot ask that his right to privacy should be measured against injury criminally done to another. But when all who are involved in the deed are consenting parties and the injury is done to morals, the public interest in the moral order can be balanced against the claims of privacy. The restriction on police powers of investigation goes further than the affording of a parallel; it means that the detection of crime committed in private and when there is no complaint is bound to be rather haphazard and this is an additional reason for moderation. These considerations do not justify the exclusion of all private immorality from the scope of the law. I think that, as I have already suggested, the test of 'private behaviour' should be substituted for 'private morality' and the influence of the factor should be reduced from that of a definite limitation to that of a matter to be taken into account. Since the gravity of the crime is also a proper consideration, a distinction might well be made in the case of homosexuality between the lesser acts of indecency and the full offence, which on the principles of the Wolfenden Report it would be illogical to do.

The last and the biggest thing to be remembered is that the law is concerned with the minimum and not with the maximum;

---

[23] (1957) Cmd. 283.

there is much in the Sermon on the Mount that would be out of place in the Ten Commandments. We all recognize the gap between the moral law and the law of the land. No man is worth much who regulates his conduct with the sole object of escaping punishment, and every worthy society sets for its members standards which are above those of the law. We recognize the existence of such higher standards when we use expressions such as 'moral obligation' and 'morally bound.' The distinction was well put in the judgement of African elders in a family dispute: 'We have power to make you divide the crops, for this is our law, and we will see this is done. But we have not power to make you behave like an upright man.'[24]

It can only be because this point is so obvious that it is so frequently ignored. Discussion among law-makers, both professional and amateur, is too often limited to what is right or wrong and good or bad for society. There is a failure to keep separate the two questions I have earlier posed—the question of society's right to pass a moral judgement and the question of whether the arm of the law should be used to enforce the judgement. The criminal law is not a statement of how people ought to behave; it is a statement of what will happen to them if they do not behave; good citizens are not expected to come within reach of it or to set their sights by it, and every enactment should be framed accordingly.

The arm of the law is an instrument to be used by society, and the decision about what particular cases it should be used in is essentially a practical one. Since it is an instrument, it is wise before deciding to use it to have regard to the tools with which it can be fitted and to the machinery which operates it. Its tools are fines, imprisonment, or lesser forms of supervision (such as Borstal and probation) and—not to be ignored—the degradation that often follows upon the publication of the crime. Are any of these suited to the job of dealing with sexual immorality? The fact that there is so much immorality which has never been brought within the law shows that there can be no general rule. It is a matter for decision in each case; but in the case of homosexuality the Wolfenden Report rightly has regard to the views of those who are experienced in dealing with this sort of crime and to those of the clergy who are the natural guardians of public morals.

The machinery which sets the criminal law in motion ends

---

[24] A case in the Saa-Katengo Kuta at Lialiu, August 1942, quoted in *The Judicial Process among the Barotse of Northern Rhodesia* by Max Gluckman, Manchester University Press, 1955, p. 172.

with the verdict and the sentence; and a verdict is given either by magistrates or by a jury. As a general rule, whenever a crime is sufficiently serious to justify a maximum punishment of more than three months, the accused has the right to the verdict of a jury. The result is that magistrates administer mostly what I have called the regulatory part of the law. They deal extensively with drunkenness, gambling, and prostitution, which are matters of morals or close to them, but not with any of the graver moral offences. They are more responsive than juries to the ideas of the legislature; it may not be accidental that the Wolfenden Report, in recommending increased penalties for solicitation, did not go above the limit of three months. Juries tend to dilute the decrees of Parliament with their own ideas of what should be punishable. Their province of course is fact and not law, and I do not mean that they often deliberately disregard the law. But if they think it is too stringent, they sometimes take a very merciful view of the facts. Let me take one example out of many that could be given. It is an offence to have carnal knowledge of a girl under the age of sixteen years. Consent on her part is no defence; if she did not consent, it would of course amount to rape. The law makes special provision for the situation when a boy and girl are near in age. If a man under twenty-four can prove that he had reasonable cause to believe that the girl was over the age of sixteen years, he has a good defence. The law regards the offence as sufficiently serious to make it one that is triable only by a judge at assizes. 'Reasonable cause' means not merely that the boy honestly believed that the girl was over sixteen but also that he must have had reasonable grounds for his belief. In theory it ought not to be an easy defence to make out but in fact it is extremely rare for anyone who advances it to be convicted. The fact is that the girl is often as much to blame as the boy. The object of the law, as judges repeatedly tell juries, is to protect young girls against themselves; but juries are not impressed.

The part that the jury plays in the enforcement of the criminal law, the fact that no grave offence against morals is punishable without their verdict, these are of great importance in relation to the statements of principle that I have been making. They turn what might otherwise be pure exhortation to the legislature into something like rules that the law-makers cannot safely ignore. The man in the jury box is not just an expression; he is an active reality. It will not in the long run work to make laws about morality that are not acceptable to him.

This then is how I believe my third interrogatory should be answered—not by the formation of hard and fast rules, but by a judgement in each case taking into account the sort of factors I have been mentioning. The line that divides the criminal law from the moral is not determinable by the application of any clear-cut principle. It is like a line that divides land and sea, a coastline of irregularities and indentations. There are gaps and promontories, such as adultery and fornication, which the law has for centuries left substantially untouched. Adultery of the sort that breaks up marriage seems to me to be just as harmful to the social fabric as homosexuality or bigamy. The only ground for putting it outside the criminal law is that a law which made it a crime would be too difficult to enforce; it is too generally regarded as a human weakness not suitably punished by imprisonment. All that the law can do with fornication is to act against its worst manifestations; there is a general abhorrence of the commercialization of vice, and that sentiment gives strength to the law against brothels and immoral earnings. There is no logic to be found in this. The boundary between the criminal law and the moral law is fixed by balancing in the case of each particular crime the pros and cons of legal enforcement in accordance with the sort of considerations I have been outlining. The fact that adultery, fornication, and lesbianism are untouched by the criminal law does not prove that homosexuality ought not to be touched. The error of jurisprudence in the Wolfenden Report is caused by the search for some single principle to explain the division between crime and sin. The Report finds it in the principle that the criminal law exists for the protection of individuals; on this principle fornication in private between consenting adults is outside the law and thus it becomes logically indefensible to bring homosexuality between consenting adults in private within it. But the true principle is that the law exists for the protection of society. It does not discharge its function by protecting the individual from injury, annoyance, corruption, and exploitation; the law must protect also the institutions and the community of ideas, political and moral, without which people cannot live together. Society cannot ignore the morality of the individual any more than it can his loyalty; it flourishes on both and without either it dies.

I have said that the morals which underlie the law must be derived from the sense of right and wrong which resides in the community as a whole; it does not matter whence the community of thought comes, whether from one body of doctrine or another or from the knowledge of good and evil which no man is without. If the reasonable man believes that a practice is immoral and believes also—no matter whether the belief is right or wrong, so be it that it is honest and dispassionate—that no right-minded member of his society could think otherwise, then for the purpose of the law it is immoral. This, you may say, makes immorality a question of fact—what the law would consider as self-evident fact no doubt, but still with no higher authority than any other doctrine of public policy. I think that that is so, and indeed the law does not distinguish between an act that is immoral and one that is contrary to public policy. But the law has never yet had occasion to inquire into the differences between Christian morals and those which every right-minded member of society is expected to hold. The inquiry would, I believe, be academic. Moralists would find differences; indeed they would find them between different branches of the Christian faith on subjects such as divorce and birth-control. But for the purpose of the limited entry which the law makes into the field of morals, there is no practical difference. It seems to me therefore that the free-thinker and the non-Christian can accept, without offence to his convictions, the fact that Christian morals are the basis of the criminal law and that he can recognize, also without taking offence, that without the support of the churches the moral order, which has its origin in and takes its strength from Christian beliefs, would collapse.

This brings me back in the end to a question I posed at the beginning. What is the relationship between crime and sin, between the Church and the Law? I do not think that you can equate crime with sin. The divine law and the secular have been disunited, but they are brought together again by the need which each has for the other. It is not my function to emphasize the Church's need of the secular law; it can be put tersely by saying that you cannot have a ceiling without a floor. I am very clear about the law's need for the Church. I have spoken of the criminal law as dealing with the minimum standards of human conduct and the moral law with the maximum. The instrument of the criminal law is punishment; those of the moral law are teaching, training, and exhortation. If the whole dead weight of sin were ever to be allowed to fall upon the law, it could not take the strain. If at any point there is a lack of clear and convincing moral teaching, the administration of the law suffers. Let me take as an illustration of this the law on abortion. I believe that a great many people nowadays do not understand why abortion is wrong. If it is right to prevent conception, at what point does it become sinful to prevent birth and why? I doubt if anyone who has not had a theological training would give a satisfactory answer to that question. Many people regard abortion as the next step when by accident birth-control has failed; and many more people are deterred from abortion not because they think it sinful or illegal but because of the difficulty which illegality puts in the way of obtaining it. The law is powerless to deal with abortion *per se;* unless a tragedy occurs or a 'professional' abortionist is involved—the parallel between the 'professional' in abortions and the 'professional' in fornication is quite close—it has to leave it alone. Without one or other of these features the crime is rarely detected; and when detected, the plea *ad misericordiam* is often too strong. The 'professional' abortionist is usually the unskilled person who for a small reward helps girls in trouble; the man and the girl involved are essential witnesses for the prosecution and therefore go free; the paid abortionist generally receives a very severe sentence, much more severe than that usually given to the paid assistant in immorality, such as the ponce or the brothel-keeper. The reason is because unskilled abortion endangers life. In a case in 1949[25] Lord Chief Justice Goddard said: 'It is because the unskilful attentions of ignorant people in cases of this kind often result in death that attempts to produce abortion are regarded by the law as very serious offences.' This gives the law a twist which disassociates it from morality and, I think, to some extent from sound sense. The act is being punished because it is dangerous, and it is dangerous largely because it is illegal and therefore performed only by the unskilled.

The object of what I have said is not to criticize theology or law in relation to abortion. That is a large subject and beyond my present scope. It is to show what happens to the law in matters of morality about which the community as a whole is not deeply imbued with a sense of sin; the law sags under a weight which it is not constructed to bear and may become permanently warped.

I return now to the main thread of my argument and summarize it. Society cannot live without morals. Its morals are those standards of conduct which the reasonable man approves. A rational man, who is also a good man, may have other standards. If he has no standards at all he is not a good man and need not be further considered. If he has standards, they may be very different; he may, for example, not disap-

25 *R.* v. *Tate, The Times,* 22 June 1949.

prove of homosexuality or abortion. In that case he will not share in the common morality; but that should not make him deny that it is a social necessity. A rebel may be rational in thinking that he is right but he is irrational if he thinks that society can leave him free to rebel.

A man who concedes that morality is necessary to society must support the use of those instruments without which morality cannot be maintained. The two instruments are those of teaching, which is doctrine, and of enforcement, which is the law. If morals could be taught simply on the basis that they are necessary to society, there would be no social need for religion; it could be left as a purely personal affair. But morality cannot be taught in that way. Loyalty is not taught in that way either. No society has yet solved the problem of how to teach morality without religion. So the law must base itself on Christian morals and to the limit of its ability enforce them, not simply because they are the morals of most of us, nor simply because they are the morals which are taught by the established Church—on these points the law recognizes the right to dissent—but for the compelling reason that without the help of Christian teaching the law will fail.

H. L. A. Hart

Immorality and Treason

The most remarkable feature of Sir Patrick's lecture is his view of the nature of morality—the morality which the criminal law may enforce. Most previous thinkers who have repudiated the liberal point of view have done so because they thought that morality consisted either of divine commands or of rational principles of human conduct discoverable by human reason. Since morality for them had this elevated divine or rational status as the law of God or reason, it seemed obvious that the state should enforce it, and that the function of human law should not be merely to provide men with the opportunity for leading a good life, but actually to see that they lead it. Sir Patrick does not rest his repudiation of the liberal point of view on these religious or rationalist conceptions. Indeed much that he writes reads like an abjuration of the notion that reasoning or thinking has much to do with morality. English popular morality has no doubt its historical connexion with the Christian religion: 'That,' says Sir Patrick, 'is how it got there.' But it does not owe its present status or social significance to religion any more than to reason.

What, then, is it? According to Sir Patrick it is primarily a matter of feeling. 'Every moral judgment,' he says, 'is a feeling that no right-minded man could act in any other way without admitting that he was doing wrong.' Who then must feel this way if we are to have what Sir Patrick calls a public morality?

H. L. A. Hart was Professor of Jurisprudence at Oxford University from 1952–1968. Since leaving the Professorship, he has been a research fellow of University College, Oxford, and also senior research fellow of the Nuffield Foundation.

Professor Hart's writing has been extremely influential in recent legal philosophy, and in contemporary Anglo-American philosophy generally. His major works include: *Causation in the Law* (with A. M. Honore) (1959); *The Concept of Law* (1961); *Law, Liberty, and Morality* (1963); and *Punishment and Responsibility* (1968).

"Immorality and Treason" originally appeared in *The Listener* (July 30, 1959), pp. 162–163, and it is reprinted here by permission of the author.

He tells us that it is 'the man in the street,' 'the man in the jury box,' or (to use the phrase so familiar to English lawyers) 'the man on the Clapham omnibus.' For the moral judgments of society so far as the law is concerned are to be ascertained by the standards of the reasonable man, and he is not to be confused with the rational man. Indeed, Sir Patrick says 'he is not expected to reason about anything and his judgment may be largely a matter of feeling.'

Intolerance, Indignation, and Disgust

But what precisely are the relevant feelings, the feelings which may justify use of the criminal law? Here the argument becomes a little complex. Widespread dislike of a practice is not enough. There must, says Sir Patrick, be 'a real feeling of reprobation.' Disgust is not enough either. What is crucial is a combination of intolerance, indignation, and disgust. These three are the forces behind the moral law, without which it is not 'weighty enough to deprive the individual of freedom of choice.' Hence there is, in Sir Patrick's outlook, a crucial difference between the mere adverse moral judgment of society and one which is inspired by feeling raised to the concert pitch of intolerance, indignation, and disgust.

This distinction is novel and also very important. For on it depends the weight to be given to the fact that when morality is enforced individual liberty is necessarily cut down. Though Sir Patrick's abstract formulation of his views on this point is hard to follow, his examples make his position fairly clear. We can see it best in the contrasting things he says about fornication and homosexuality. In regard to fornication, public feeling in most societies is not now of the concert-pitch intensity. We may feel that it is tolerable if confined: only its spread might be gravely injurious. In such cases the question whether individual liberty should be restricted is for Sir Patrick a question of balance between the danger to society in the one scale, and the restriction of the individual in the other. But if, as may be the case with homosexuality, public feeling is up to concert pitch, if it expresses a 'deliberate judgment' that a practice as such is injurious to society, if there is 'a genuine feeling that it is a vice so abominable that its mere presence is an offence,' then it is beyond the limits of tolerance, and society may eradicate it. In this case, it seems, no further balancing of the claims of individual liberty is to be done, though as a matter of prudence the legislator should remember that the popular limits of tolerance may shift: the concert pitch feeling may subside. This may produce a dilemma for the law; for the law may then be left without the full moral backing that it needs, yet it cannot be altered without giving the impression that the moral judgment is being weakened.

A Shared Morality

If this is what morality is—a compound of indignation, intolerance, and disgust—we may well ask what justification there is for taking it, and turning it as such, into criminal law with all the misery which criminal punishment entails. Here Sir Patrick's answer is very clear and simple. A collection of individuals is not a society; what makes them into a society is among other things a shared or public morality. This is as necessary to its existence as an organized government. So society may use the law to preserve its morality like anything else essential to it. 'The suppression of vice is as much the law's business as the suppression of subversive activities.' The liberal point of view which denies this is guilty of 'an error in jurisprudence': for it is no more possible to define an area of private morality than an area of private subversive activity. There can be no 'theoretical limits' to legislation against immorality just as there are no such limits to the power of the state to legislate against treason and sedition.

Surely all this, ingenious as it is, is misleading. Mill's formulation of the liberal point of view may well be too simple. The grounds for interfering with human liberty are more various than the single criterion of 'harm to others' suggests: cruelty to animals or organizing prostitution for gain do not, as Mill himself saw, fall easily under the description of harm to others. Conversely, even where there is harm to others in the most literal sense, there may well be other principles limiting the extent to which harmful activities should be repressed by law. So there are multiple criteria, not a single criterion, determining when human liberty may be restricted. Perhaps this is what Sir Patrick means by a curious distinction which he often stresses between theoretical and practical limits. But with all its simplicities the liberal point of view is a better guide than Sir Patrick to clear thought on the proper relation of morality to the criminal law: for it stresses what he obscures—namely, the points at which thought is needed before we turn popular morality into criminal law.

Society and Moral Opinion

No doubt we would all agree that a consensus of moral opinion on certain matters is essential if society is to be worth living in. Laws against murder, theft, and much else would be of little use if they were not supported by a widely diffused conviction that what these laws forbid is also immoral. So much is obvious. But it does not follow that everything to which the moral vetoes of accepted morality attach is of equal importance to society; nor is there the slightest reason for thinking of morality as a seamless web: one which will fall to pieces carrying society with it, unless all its emphatic vetoes are enforced by law. Surely even in the face of the moral feeling that is up to concert pitch—the trio of intolerance, indignation, and disgust—we must pause to think. We must ask a question at two different levels which Sir Patrick never clearly enough identifies or separates. First, we must ask whether a practice which offends moral feeling is harmful, independently of its repercussion on the general moral code. Secondly, what about repercussion on the moral code? Is it really true that failure to translate this item of general morality into criminal law will jeopardize the whole fabric of morality and so of society?

We cannot escape thinking about these two different questions merely by repeating to ourselves the vague nostrum: 'This is part of public morality and public morality must be preserved if society is to exist.' Sometimes Sir Patrick seems to admit this, for he says in words which both Mill and the Wolfenden Report might have used, that there must be the maximum respect for individual liberty consistent with the integrity of society. Yet this, as his contrasting examples of fornication and homosexuality show, turns out to mean only that the immorality which the law may punish must be generally felt to be intolerable. This plainly is no adequate substitute for a reasoned estimate of the damage to the fabric of society likely to ensue if it is not suppressed.

Nothing perhaps shows more clearly the inadequacy of Sir Patrick's approach to this problem than his comparison between the suppression of sexual immorality and the suppression of treason or subversive activity. Private subversive activity is, of course, a contradiction in terms because 'subversion' means overthrowing government, which is a public thing. But it is grotesque, even where moral feeling against homosexuality is up to concert pitch, to think of the homosexual behaviour of two adults in private as in any way like treason or sedition either in intention or effect. We can make it *seem* like treason only if we assume that deviation from a general moral code is bound to affect that code, and to lead not merely to its modification but to its destruction. The analogy could begin to be plausible only if it was clear that offending against this item of morality was likely to jeopardize the whole structure. But we have ample evidence for believing that people will not abandon morality, will not think any better of murder, cruelty, and dishonesty, merely because some private sexual practice which they abominate is not punished by the law.

Because this is so the analogy with treason is absurd. Of course 'No man is an island': what one man does in private, if it is known, may affect others in many different ways. Indeed it may be that deviation from general sexual morality by those whose lives, like the lives of many homosexuals, are noble ones and in all other ways exemplary will lead to what Sir Patrick calls the shifting of the limits of tolerance. But if this has any analogy in the sphere of government it is not the overthrow of ordered government, but a peaceful change in its form. So we may listen to the promptings of common sense and of logic, and say that though there could not logically be a sphere of private treason there is a sphere of private morality and immorality.

Sir Patrick's doctrine is also open to a wider, perhaps a deeper, criticism. In his reaction against a rationalist morality and his stress on feeling, he has I think thrown out the baby and kept the bath water; and the bath water may turn out to be very dirty indeed. When Sir Patrick's lecture was first delivered *The Times* greeted it with these words: 'There is a moving and welcome humility in the conception that society should not be asked to give its reason for refusing to tolerate what in its heart it feels intolerable.' This drew from a correspondent in Cambridge the retort: 'I am afraid that we are less humble than we used to be. We once burnt old women because, without giving our reasons, we felt in our hearts that witchcraft was intolerable.'

This retort is a bitter one, yet its bitterness is salutary. We are not, I suppose, likely, in England, to take again to the burning of old women for witchcraft or to punishing people for associating with those of a different race or colour, or to punishing people again for adultery. Yet if these things were viewed with intolerance, indignation, and disgust, as the second of them still is in some countries, it seems that on Sir

Patrick's principles no rational criticism could be opposed to the claim that they should be punished by law. We could only pray, in his words, that the limits of tolerance might shift.

Curious Logic

It is impossible to see what curious logic has led Sir Patrick to this result. For him a practice is immoral if the thought of it makes the man on the Clapham omnibus sick. So be it. Still, why should we not summon all the resources of our reason, sympathetic understanding, as well as critical intelligence, and insist that before general moral feeling is turned into criminal law it is submitted to scrutiny of a different kind from Sir Patrick's? Surely, the legislator should ask whether the general morality is based on ignorance, superstition, or misunderstanding; whether there is a false conception that those who practise what it condemns are in other ways dangerous or hostile to society; and whether the misery to many parties, the blackmail and the other evil consequences of criminal punishment, especially for sexual offences, are well understood. It is surely extraordinary that among the things which Sir Patrick says are to be considered before we legislate against immorality these appear nowhere; not even as 'practical considerations,' let alone 'theoretical limits.' To any theory which, like this one, asserts that the criminal law may be used on the vague ground that the preservation of morality is essential to society and yet omits to stress the need for critical scrutiny, our reply should be: 'Morality, what crimes may be committed in thy name!'

As Mill saw, and de Tocqueville showed in detail long ago in his critical but sympathetic study of democracy, it is fatally easy to confuse the democratic principle that power should be in the hands of the majority with the utterly different claim that the majority, with power in their hands, need respect no limits. Certainly there is a special risk in a democracy that the majority may dictate how all should live. This is the risk we run, and should gladly run; for it is the price of all that is so good in democratic rule. But loyalty to democratic principles does not require us to maximize this risk: yet this is what we shall do if we mount the man in the street on the top of the Clapham omnibus and tell him that if only he feels sick enough about what other people do in private to demand its suppression by law no theoretical criticism can be made of his demand.

Ronald Dworkin

Lord Devlin and the Enforcement of Morals

. . . There are two chief arguments [in Lord Devlin's book, *The Enforcement of Morals*]. The first is set out in structured form in the Maccabaean Lecture. It argues from society's right to protect its own existence. The second, a quite different and much more important argument, develops in disjointed form through various essays. It argues from the majority's right to follow its own moral convictions in defending its social environment from change it opposes. I shall consider these two arguments in turn, but the second at greater length.

The First Argument: Society's Right to Protect Itself

The first argument—and the argument which has received by far the major part of the critics' attention—is this:[1]

(1) In a modern society there are a variety of moral principles which some men adopt for their own guidance and do not attempt to impose upon others. There are also moral standards which the majority places beyond toleration and imposes upon those who dissent. For us, the dictates of particular religion are an example of the former class, and the practice of monogamy an example of the latter. A society cannot survive unless some standards are of the second class, because some moral conformity is essential to its life. Every society has a

Ronald Dworkin was a professor of law at the Yale Law School until the fall of 1969, at which time he left Yale to succeed H. L. A. Hart as Professor of Jurisprudence at Oxford University. Professor Dworkin has written a number of important essays in the field of legal philosophy, including "The Model of Rules," U. of Chicago Law Review, Vol. 35, p. 140.

The article presented here is reprinted by permission of the author, The Yale Law Journal Company, and Fred B. Rothman and Company from *The Yale Law Journal*, Vol. 75, p. 986.

[1] It is developed chiefly in Devlin, *The Enforcement of Morals*, pp. 7–25.

right to preserve its own existence, and therefore the right to insist on some such conformity.

(2) If society has such a right, then it has the right to use the institutions and sanctions of its criminal law to enforce the right—"[S]ociety may use the law to preserve morality in the same way it uses it to safeguard anything else if it is essential to its existence."[2] Just as society may use its law to prevent treason, it may use it to prevent a corruption of that conformity which ties it together.

(3) But society's right to punish immorality by law should not necessarily be exercised against every sort and on every occasion of immorality—we must recognize the impact and the importance of some restraining principles. There are several of these, but the most important is that there "must be toleration of the maximum individual freedom that is consistent with the integrity of society."[3] These restraining principles, taken together, require that we exercise caution in concluding that a practice is considered profoundly immoral. The law should stay its hand if it detects any uneasiness or half-heartedness or latent toleration in society's condemnation of the practice. But none of these restraining principles apply, and hence society is free to enforce its rights, when public feeling is high, enduring and relentless, when, in Lord Devlin's phrase, it rises to "intolerance, indignation and disgust."[4] Hence the summary conclusion about homosexuality: if it is genuinely regarded as an abominable vice, society's right to eradicate it cannot be denied.

We must guard against a possible, indeed tempting, misconception of this argument. It does not depend upon any assumption that when the vast bulk of a community thinks a practice is immoral they are likely right. What Lord Devlin thinks is at stake, when our public morality is challenged, is the very survival of society, and he believes that society is entitled to preserve itself without vouching for the morality that holds it together.

Is this argument sound? Professor H. L. A. Hart, responding to its appearance at the heart of the Maccabaean lecture,[5] thought that it rested upon a confused conception of what a society is. If one holds anything like a conventional notion of a society, he said, it is absurd to suggest that every practice

2 *Ibid.*, p. 11.
3 *Ibid.*, p. 16.
4 *Ibid.*, p. 17.
5 H. L. A. Hart, *Law, Liberty and Morality* (1963), p. 51.

the society views as profoundly immoral and disgusting threatens its survival. This is as silly as arguing that society's existence is threatened by the death of one of its members or the birth of another, and Lord Devlin, he reminds us, offers nothing by way of evidence to support any such claim. But if one adopts an artificial definition of a society, such that a society consists of that particular complex of moral ideas and attitudes which its members happen to hold at a particular moment in time, it is intolerable that each such moral status quo should have the right to preserve its precarious existence by force. So, Professor Hart argued, Lord Devlin's argument fails whether a conventional or an artificial sense of "society" is taken.

Lord Devlin replies to Professor Hart in a new and lengthy footnote. After summarizing Hart's criticism he comments, "I do not assert that *any* deviation from a society's shared morality threatens its existence any more than I assert that *any* subversive activity threatens its existence. I assert that they are both activities which are capable in their nature of threatening the existence of society so that neither can be put beyond the law."[6] This reply exposes a serious flaw in the architecture of the argument.

It tells us that we must understand the second step of the argument—the crucial claim that society has a right to enforce its public morality by law—as limited to a denial of the proposition that society never has such a right. Lord Devlin apparently understood the Wolfenden Report's statement of a "realm of private morality . . . not the law's business" to assert a fixed jurisdictional barrier placing private sexual practices forever beyond the law's scrutiny. His arguments, the new footnote tells us, are designed to show merely that no such constitutional barrier should be raised, because it is possible that the challenge to established morality might be so profound that the very existence of a conformity in morals, and hence of the society itself, would be threatened.[7]

---

[6] Devlin, p. 13.

[7] This reading had great support in the text even without the new footnote: "I think, therefore, that it is not possible to set theoretical limits to the power of the State to legislate against immorality. It is not possible to settle in advance exceptions to the general rule or to define inflexibly areas of morality into which the law is in no circumstances to be allowed to enter." [Devlin, pp. 12–13.] The arguments presented bear out this construction. They are of the *reductio ad absurdum* variety, exploiting the possibility that what is immoral can in theory become subversive of society. "But suppose a quarter or a half of the population got drunk every night, what sort of society would it be? You cannot set a theoretical limit to the number of people who can get drunk before society is entitled to legislate against

We might well remain unconvinced, even of this limited point. We might believe that the danger which any unpopular practice can present to the existence of society is so small that it would be wise policy, a prudent protection of individual liberty from transient hysteria, to raise just this sort of constitutional barrier and forbid periodic reassessments of the risk.

But if we were persuaded to forego this constitutional barrier we would expect the third step in the argument to answer the inevitable next question: Granted that a challenge to deep-seated and genuine public morality may conceivably threaten society's existence, and so must be placed above the threshold of the law's concern, how shall we know when the danger is sufficiently clear and present to justify not merely scrutiny but action? What more is needed beyond the fact of passionate public disapproval to show that we are in the presence of an actual threat?

The rhetoric of the third step makes it seem responsive to this question—there is much talk of "freedom" and "toleration" and even "balancing." But the argument is not responsive, for freedom, toleration and balancing turn out to be appropriate only when the public outrage diagnosed at the second step is shown to be overstated, when the fever, that is, turns out to be feigned. When the fever is confirmed, when the intolerance, indignation and disgust are genuine, the principle that calls for "the maximum individual freedom consistent with the integrity of society" no longer applies. But this means that nothing more than passionate public disapproval is necessary after all.

In short, the argument involves an intellectual sleight of hand. At the second step, public outrage is presented as a threshold criterion, merely placing the practice in a category which the law is not forbidden to regulate. But offstage, somewhere in the transition to the third step, this threshold criterion becomes itself a dispositive affirmative reason for action, so

---

drunkenness. The same may be said of gambling." [*Ibid.*, p. 14.] Each example argues that no jurisdictional limit may be drawn, not that every drunk or every act of gambling threatens society. There is no suggestion that society is entitled actually to make drunkenness or gambling crimes if the practice in fact falls below the level of danger. Indeed Lord Devlin quotes the Royal Commission on Betting, Lotteries, and Gaming to support his example on gambling: "If we were convinced that whatever the degree of gambling this effect [on the character of the gambler as a member of society] must be harmful we should be inclined to think that it was the duty of the state to restrict gambling to the greatest extent practicable." [Cmd. No. 8190 at para. 159 (1951), quoted in Devlin, p. 14.] The implication is that society may scrutinize and be ready to regulate, but should not actually do so until the threat of harm in fact exists.

that when it is clearly met the law may proceed without more. The power of this manoeuvre is proved by the passage on homosexuality. Lord Devlin concludes that if our society hates homosexuality enough it is justified in outlawing it, and forcing human beings to choose between the miseries of frustration and persecution, because of the danger the practice presents to society's existence. He manages this conclusion without offering evidence that homosexuality presents any danger at all to society's existence, beyond the naked claim that all "deviations from a society's shared morality . . . are capable in their nature of threatening the existence of society" and so "cannot be put beyond the law."[8]

The Second Argument: Society's Right to Follow Its Own Lights

We are therefore justified in setting aside the first argument and turning to the second. My reconstruction includes making a great deal explicit which I believe implicit, and so involves some risk of distortion, but I take the second argument to be this:[9]

(1) If those who have homosexual desires freely indulged them, our social environment would change. What the changes would be cannot be calculated with any precision, but it is plausible to suppose, for example, that the position of the family, as the assumed and natural institution around which the educational, economic and recreational arrangements of men center, would be undermined, and the further ramifications of that would be great. We are too sophisticated to suppose that the effects of an increase in homosexuality would be confined to those who participate in the practice alone, just as we are too sophisticated to suppose that prices and wages affect only those who negotiate them. The environment in which we and our children must live is determined, among other things, by patterns and relationships formed privately by others than ourselves.

(2) This in itself does not give society the right to prohibit homosexual practices. We cannot conserve every custom we like by jailing those who do not want to preserve it. But it

---

[8] Devlin, p. 13, n.1.

[9] Most of the argument appears in Devlin, chapters V, VI and VII. See also an article published after the book: *Law and Morality,* 1 Manitoba L.S.J. 243 (1964/65).

means that our legislators must inevitably decide some moral issues. They must decide whether the institutions which seem threatened are sufficiently valuable to protect at the cost of human freedom. And they must decide whether the practices which threaten that institution are immoral, for if they are then the freedom of an individual to pursue them counts for less. We do not need so strong a justification, in terms of the social importance of the institutions being protected, if we are confident that no one has a moral right to do what we want to prohibit. We need less of a case, that is, to abridge someone's freedom to lie, cheat or drive recklessly, than his freedom to choose his own jobs or to price his own goods. This does not claim that immorality is sufficient to make conduct criminal; it argues, rather, that on occasion it is necessary.

(3) But how shall a legislator decide whether homosexual acts are immoral? Science can give no answer, and a legislator can no longer properly turn to organized religion. If it happens, however, that the vast bulk of the community is agreed upon an answer, even though a small minority of educated men may dissent, the legislator has a duty to act on the consensus. He has such a duty for two closely connected reasons: (a) In the last analysis the decision must rest on some article of moral faith, and in a democracy this sort of issue, above all others, must be settled in accordance with democratic principles. (b) It is, after all, the community which acts when the threats and sanctions of the criminal law are brought to bear. The community must take the moral responsibility, and it must therefore act on its own lights—that is, on the moral faith of its members.

This, as I understand it, is Lord Devlin's second argument. It is complex, and almost every component invites analysis and challenge. Some readers will dissent from its central assumption, that a change in social institutions is the sort of harm a society is entitled to protect itself against. Others who do not take this strong position (perhaps because they approve of laws which are designed to protect economic institutions) will nevertheless feel that society is not entitled to act, however immoral the practice, unless the threatened harm to an institution is demonstrable and imminent rather than speculative. Still others will challenge the thesis that the morality or immorality of an act ought even to count in determining whether to make it criminal (though they would no doubt admit that it does count under present practice), and others still will argue that even in a democracy legislators have the duty to decide moral questions for themselves, and must not refer such issues to the community at large. I do not propose to argue now for or against any of these positions. I want instead to consider whether Lord Devlin's conclusions are valid on his own terms, on the assumption, that is, that society does have a right to protect its central and valued social institutions against conduct which the vast bulk of its members disapproves on moral principle.

I shall argue that his conclusions are not valid, even on these terms, because he misunderstands what it is to disapprove on moral principle. I might say a cautionary word about the argument I shall present. It will consist in part of reminders that certain types of moral language (terms like "prejudice" and "moral position," for example) have standard uses in moral argument. My purpose is not to settle issues of political morality by the fiat of a dictionary, but to exhibit what I believe to be mistakes in Lord Devlin's moral sociology. I shall try to show that our conventional moral practices are more complex and more structured than he takes them to be, and that he consequently misunderstands what it means to say that the criminal law should be drawn from public morality. This is a popular and appealing thesis, and it lies near the core not only of Lord Devlin's, but of many other, theories about law and morals. It is crucial that its implications be understood.

The Concept of a Moral Position

We might start with the fact that terms like "moral position" and "moral conviction" function in our conventional morality as terms of justification and criticism, as well as of description. It is true that we sometimes speak of a group's "morals," or "morality," or "moral beliefs," or "moral positions," or "moral convictions," in what might be called an anthropological sense, meaning to refer to whatever attitudes the group displays about the propriety of human conduct, qualities or goals. We say, in this sense, that the morality of Nazi Germany was based on prejudice, or was irrational. But we also use some of these terms, particularly "moral position" and "moral conviction," in a discriminatory sense, to contrast the positions they describe with prejudices, rationalizations, matters of personal aversion or taste, arbitrary stands, and the like. One use—perhaps the most characteristic use—of this discriminatory sense is to offer a limited but important sort of justification for an act, when the moral issues surrounding that act are unclear or in dispute.

Suppose I tell you that I propose to vote against a man

running for a public office of trust because I know him to be a homosexual and because I believe that homosexuality is profoundly immoral. If you disagree that homosexuality is immoral, you may accuse me of being about to cast my vote unfairly, acting on prejudice or out of a personal repugnance which is irrelevant to the moral issue. I might then try to convert you to my position on homosexuality, but if I fail in this I shall still want to convince you of what you and I will both take to be a separate point—that my vote was based upon *a* moral position, in the discriminatory sense, even though one which differs from yours. I shall want to persuade you of this, because if I do I am entitled to expect that you will alter your opinion of me and of what I am about to do. Your judgment of my character will be different—you might still think me eccentric (or puritanical or unsophisticated) but these are types of character and not faults of character. Your judgment of my act will also be different, in this respect. You will admit that so long as I hold my moral position, I have a moral right to vote against the homosexual, because I have a right (indeed a duty) to vote my own convictions. You would not admit such a right (or duty) if you were still persuaded that I was acting out of a prejudice or a personal taste.

I am entitled to expect that your opinion will change in these ways, because these distinctions are a part of the conventional morality you and I share, and which forms the background for our discussion. They enforce the difference between positions we must respect, although we think them wrong, and positions we need not respect because they offend some ground rule of moral reasoning. A great deal of debate about moral issues (in real life, although not in philosophy texts) consists of arguments that some position falls on one or the other side of this crucial line.

It is this feature of conventional morality that animates Lord Devlin's argument that society has the right to follow its own lights. We must therefore examine that discriminatory concept of a moral position more closely, and we can do so by pursuing our imaginary conversation. What must I do to convince you that my position is a moral position?

(a) I must produce some reasons for it. This is not to say that I have to articulate a moral principle I am following or a general moral theory to which I subscribe. Very few people can do either, and the ability to hold a moral position is not limited to those who can. My reason need not be a principle or theory at all. It must only point out some aspect or feature of homosexuality which moves me to regard it as immoral: the fact that the Bible forbids it, for example, or that one who practices homosexuality becomes unfit for marriage and parenthood. Of course, any such reason would presuppose my acceptance of some general principle or theory, but I need not be able to state what it is, or realize that I am relying upon it.

Not every reason I might give will do, however. Some will be excluded by general criteria stipulating sorts of reasons which do not count. We might take note of four of the most important such criteria:

(i) If I tell you that homosexuals are morally inferior because they do not have heterosexual desires, and so are not "real men," you would reject that reason as showing one type of prejudice. Prejudices, in general, are postures of judgment that take into account considerations our conventions exclude. In a structured context, like a trial or a contest, the ground rules exclude all but certain considerations, and a prejudice is a basis of judgment which violates these rules. Our conventions stipulate some ground rules of moral judgment which obtain even apart from such special contexts, the most important of which is that a man must not be held morally inferior on the basis of some physical, racial or other characteristic he cannot help having. Thus a man whose moral judgments about Jews, or Negroes, or Southerners, or women, or effeminate men are based on his belief that any member of these classes automatically deserves less respect, without regard to anything he himself has done, is said to be prejudiced against that group.

(ii) If I base my view about homosexuals on a personal emotional reaction ("they make me sick") you would reject that reason as well. We distinguish moral positions from emotional reactions, not because moral positions are supposed to be unemotional or dispassionate—quite the reverse is true—but because the moral position is supposed to justify the emotional reaction, and not vice versa. If a man is unable to produce such reasons, we do not deny the fact of his emotional involvement, which may have important social or political consequences, but we do not take this involvement as demonstrating his moral conviction. Indeed, it is just this sort of position—a severe emotional reaction to a practice or a situation for which one cannot account—that we tend to describe, in lay terms, as a phobia or an obsession.

(iii) If I base my position on a proposition of fact ("homosexual acts are physically debilitating") which is not only false, but is so implausible that it challenges the minimal standards of evidence and argument I generally accept and impose upon others, then you would regard my belief, even though sincere, as a form of rationalization, and disqualify my reason on that ground. (Rationalization is a complex concept, and also includes, as we shall see, the production of reasons which suggest general theories I do not accept.)

(iv) If I can argue for my own position only by citing the beliefs of others ("everyone knows homosexuality is a sin") you will conclude that I am parroting and not relying on a moral conviction of my own. With the possible (though complex) exception of a deity, there is no moral authority to which I can appeal and so automatically make my position a moral one. I must have my own reasons, though of course I may have been taught these reasons by others.

No doubt many readers will disagree with these thumbnail sketches of prejudice, mere emotional reaction, rationalization and parroting. Some may have their own theories of what these are. I want to emphasize now only that these are distinct concepts, whatever the details of the differences might be, and that they have a role in deciding whether to treat another's position as a moral conviction. They are not merely epithets to be pasted on positions we strongly dislike.

(b) Suppose I do produce a reason which is not disqualified on one of these (or on similar) grounds. That reason will presuppose some general moral principle or theory, even though I may not be able to state that principle or theory, and do not have it in mind when I speak. If I offer, as my reason, the fact that the Bible forbids homosexual acts, or that homosexual acts make it less likely that the actor will marry and raise children, I suggest that I accept the theory my reason presupposes, and you will not be satisfied that my position is a moral one if you believe that I do not. It may be a question of my sincerity—do I in fact believe that the injunctions of the Bible are morally binding as such, or that all men have a duty to procreate? Sincerity is not, however, the only issue, for consistency is also in point. I may believe that I accept one of these general positions, and be wrong, because my other beliefs, and my own conduct on other occasions, may be inconsistent with it. I may reject certain Biblical injunctions, or I may hold that men have a right to remain bachelors if they please or use contraceptives all their lives.

Of course, my general moral positions may have qualifications and exceptions. The difference between an exception and an inconsistency is that the former can be supported by reasons which presuppose other moral positions I can properly claim to hold. Suppose I condemn all homosexuals on Biblical authority, but not all fornicators. What reason can I offer for the distinction? If I can produce none which supports it, I cannot claim to accept the general position about Biblical authority. If I do produce a reason which seems to support the distinction, the same sorts of question may be asked about that reason as were asked about my original reply. What general position does the reason for my exception presuppose? Can I sincerely claim to accept that further general position? Suppose my reason, for example, is that fornication is now very common, and has been sanctioned by custom. Do I really believe that what is immoral becomes moral when it becomes popular? If not, and if I can produce no other reason for the distinction, I cannot claim to accept the general position that what the Bible condemns is immoral. Of course, I may be persuaded, when this is pointed out, to change my views on fornication. But you would be alert to the question of whether this is a genuine change of heart, or only a performance for the sake of the argument.

In principle there is no limit to these ramifications of my original claim, though of course, no actual argument is likely to pursue very many of them.

(c) But do I really have to have a reason to make my position a matter of moral conviction? Most men think that acts which cause unnecessary suffering, or break a serious promise with no excuse, are immoral, and yet they could give no reason for these beliefs. They feel that no reason is necessary, because they take it as axiomatic or self-evident that these are immoral acts. It seems contrary to common sense to deny that a position held in this way can be a moral position.

Yet there is an important difference between believing that one's position is self-evident and just not having a reason for one's position. The former presupposes a positive belief that no further reason is necessary, that the immorality of the act in question does not depend upon its social effects, or its effects on the character of the actor, or its proscription by a deity, or anything else, but follows from the nature of the act itself. The claim that a particular position is axiomatic, in other words, does supply a reason of a special sort, namely that the act is immoral in and of itself, and this special reason, like the others we considered, may be inconsistent with more general theories I hold.

The moral arguments we make presuppose not only moral principles, but also more abstract positions about moral reasoning. In particular, they presuppose positions about what kinds of acts can be immoral in and of themselves. When I criticize your moral opinions, or attempt to justify my own disregard of traditional moral rules I think are silly, I will likely proceed by denying that the act in question has any of the several features that can make an act immoral—that it involves no breach of an undertaking or duty, for example, harms no one including the actor, is not proscribed by any organized religion, and is not illegal. I proceed in this way because I assume that the ultimate grounds of immorality are limited to some such small set of very general standards. I may assert this assumption directly or it may emerge from the pattern of my argument. In either event, I will enforce it by calling positions which can claim no support from any of these ultimate standards *arbitrary,* as I should certainly do if you said that photography was immoral, for instance, or swimming. Even if I cannot articulate this underlying assumption, I shall still apply it, and since the ultimate criteria I recognize are among the most abstract of my moral standards, they will not vary much from those my neighbors recognize and apply. Although many who despise homosexuals are unable to say why, few would claim affirmatively that one needs no reason, for this would make their position, on their own standards, an arbitrary one.

(d) This anatomy of our argument could be continued, but it is already long enough to justify some conclusions. If the issue between us is whether my views on homosexuality amount to a moral position, and hence whether I am entitled to vote against a homosexual on that ground, I cannot settle the issue simply by reporting my feelings. You will want to consider the reasons I can produce to support my belief, and whether my other views and behavior are consistent with the theories these reasons presuppose. You will have, of course, to apply your own understanding, which may differ in detail from mine, of what a prejudice or a rationalization is, for example, and of when one view is inconsistent with another. You and I may end in disagreement over whether my position is a moral one, partly because one is less likely to recognize these illegitimate grounds in himself than in others.

We must avoid the sceptical fallacy of passing from these facts to the conclusion that there is no such thing as a prejudice or a rationalization or an inconsistency, or that these terms mean merely that the one who uses them strongly dislikes the positions he describes this way. That would be like arguing that because different people have different understandings of what jealousy is, and can in good faith disagree about whether one of them is jealous, there is no such thing as jealousy, and one who says another is jealous merely means he dislikes him very much.

Lord Devlin's Morality

We may now return to Lord Devlin's second argument. He argues that when legislators must decide a moral issue (as by his hypothesis they must when a practice threatens a valued social arrangement), they must follow any consensus of moral position which the community at large has reached, because this is required by the democratic principle, and because a community is entitled to follow its own lights. The argument would have some plausibility if Lord Devlin meant, in speaking of the moral consensus of the community, those positions which are moral positions in the discriminatory sense we have been exploring.

But he means nothing of the sort. His definition of a moral position shows he is using it in what I called the anthropological sense. The ordinary man whose opinions we must enforce, he says, ". . . is not expected to reason about anything and his judgment may be largely a matter of feeling."[10] "If the reasonable man believes," he adds, "that a practice is immoral and believes also—no matter whether the belief is right or wrong, so be it that it is honest and dispassionate—that no right-minded member of his society could think otherwise, then for the purpose of the law it is immoral."[11] Elsewhere he quotes with approval Dean Rostow's attribution to him of the view that "the common morality of a society at any time is a blend of custom and conviction, of reason and feeling, of experience and prejudice."[12] His sense of what a moral conviction is emerges most clearly of all from the famous remark about homosexuals. If the ordinary man regards homosexuality "as a vice so abominable that its mere presence is an offence,"[13] this demonstrates for him that the ordinary man's feelings about homosexuals are a matter of moral conviction.[14]

[10] Devlin, 15.

[11] *Ibid.*, pp. 22–23.

[12] Rostow, *The Enforcement of Morals,* 1960 Camb. L.J. 174, 197; reprinted in E. V. Rostow, *The Sovereign Prerogative* 45, 78 (1962). Quoted in Devlin 95.

[13] *Ibid.*, p. 17.

[14] In the preface (*Ibid.*, p. viii) Lord Devlin acknowledges that the language of the original lecture might have placed "too much emphasis on feeling and too little on reason," and he states that the legislator is entitled to disregard "irrational" beliefs. He gives as an example of the latter the belief

His conclusions fail because they depend upon using "moral position" in this anthropological sense. Even if it is true that most men think homosexuality an abominable vice and cannot tolerate its presence, it remains possible that this common opinion is a compound of prejudice (resting on the assumption that homosexuals are morally inferior creatures because they are effeminate), rationalization (based on assumptions of fact so unsupported that they challenge the community's own standards of rationality), and personal aversion (representing no conviction but merely blind hate rising from unacknowledged self-suspicion). It remains possible that the ordinary man could produce no reason for his view, but would simply parrot his neighbor who in turn parrots him, or that he would produce a reason which presupposes a general moral position he could not sincerely or consistently claim to hold. If so, the principles of democracy we follow do not call for the enforcement of the consensus, for the belief that prejudices, personal aversions and rationalizations do not justify restricting another's freedom itself occupies a critical and fundamental position in our popular morality. Nor would the bulk of the community then be entitled to follow its own lights, for the community does not extend that privilege to one who acts on the basis of prejudice, rationalization, or personal aversion. Indeed, the distinction between these and moral convictions, in the discriminatory sense, exists largely to mark off the former as the sort of positions one is not entitled to pursue.

A conscientious legislator who is told a moral consensus exists must test the credentials of that consensus. He cannot, of course, examine the beliefs or behavior of individual citizens; he cannot hold hearings on the Clapham omnibus. That is not the point.

The claim that a moral consensus exists is not itself based on a poll. It is based on an appeal to the legislator's sense of how his community reacts to some disfavored practice. But this same sense includes an awareness of the grounds on which that reaction is generally supported. If there has been a public debate involving the editorial columns, speeches of his colleagues, the testimony of interested groups, and his

---

that homosexuality causes earthquakes, and asserts that the exclusion of irrationality "is usually an easy and comparatively unimportant process." I think it fair to conclude that this is all Lord Devlin would allow him to exclude. If I am wrong, and Lord Devlin would ask him to exclude prejudices, personal aversions, arbitrary stands and the rest as well, he should have said so, and attempted to work some of these distinctions out. If he had, his conclusions would have been different and would no doubt have met with a different reaction.

own correspondence, these will sharpen his awareness of what arguments and positions are in the field. He must sift these arguments and positions, trying to determine which are prejudices or rationalizations, which presuppose general principles or theories vast parts of the population could not be supposed to accept, and so on. It may be that when he has finished this process of reflection he will find that the claim of a moral consensus has not been made out. In the case of homosexuality, I expect, it would not be, and that is what makes Lord Devlin's undiscriminating hypothetical so serious a misstatement. What is shocking and wrong is not his idea that the community's morality counts, but his idea of what counts as the community's morality.

Of course the legislator must apply these tests for himself. If he shares the popular views he is less likely to find them wanting, though if he is self-critical the exercise may convert him. His answer, in any event, will depend upon his own understanding of what our shared morality requires. That is inevitable, for whatever criteria we urge him to apply, he can apply them only as he understands them.

A legislator who proceeds in this way, who refuses to take popular indignation, intolerance and disgust as the moral conviction of his community, is not guilty of moral elitism. He is not simply setting his own educated views against those of a vast public which rejects them. He is doing his best to enforce a distinct, and fundamentally important, part of his community's morality, a consensus more essential to society's existence in the form we know it than the opinion Lord Devlin bids him follow.

No legislator can afford to ignore the public's outrage. It is a fact he must reckon with. It will set the boundaries of what is politically feasible, and it will determine his strategies of persuasion and enforcement within these boundaries. But we must not confuse strategy with justice, nor facts of political life with principles of political morality. Lord Devlin understands these distinctions, but his arguments will appeal most, I am afraid, to those who do not.

Postscript on Pornography

I have been discussing homosexuality because that is Lord Devlin's example. I should like to say a word about pornography, if only because it is, for the time being, more in the American legal headlines than homosexuality. This current attention is due to the Supreme Court's decision and opinions in three recent cases: *Ginzburg, Mishkin* and *Fanny Hill.*[15] In two of these, convictions (and jail sentences) for the distribution of pornography were upheld, and in the third, while the Court reversed a state ban on an allegedly obscene novel, three justices dissented.

Two of the cases involved review of state procedures for constitutionality, and the third the interpretation and application of a federal statute. The Court therefore had to pass on the constitutional question of how far a state or the nation may legally restrict the publication of erotic literature, and on questions of statutory construction. But each decision nevertheless raises issues of political principle of the sort we have been considering.

A majority of the Court adheres to the constitutional test laid down some years ago in *Roth.*[16] As that test now stands, a book is obscene, and as such not protected by the first amendment, if: "(a) the dominant theme of the material taken as a whole appeals to a prurient interest in sex; (b) the material is patently offensive because it affronts contemporary community standards relating to the description or representation of sexual matters; and (c) the material is utterly without redeeming social value."[17] We might put the question of political principle this way: What gives the federal government, or any state, the moral right to prohibit the publication of books which are obscene under the *Roth* test?

Justice Brennan's opinion in *Mishkin* floated one answer: erotic literature, he said, incites some readers to crime. If this is true, if in a significant number of such cases the same readers would not have been incited to the same crime by other stimuli, and if the problem cannot effectively be handled in other ways, this might give society a warrant to ban these books. But these are at least speculative hypotheses, and in any event they are not pertinent to a case like *Ginzburg,* in which the Court based its decision not on the obscene character of the publications themselves, but on the fact that they were presented to the public as salacious rather than enlightening. Can any other justification be given for the prohibition of obscene books?

[15] Ginzburg v. United States, 383 U.S. 463 (1966); Mishkin v. New York, 383 U.S. 502 (1966); Memoirs v. Massachusetts (Fanny Hill), 383 U.S. 413 (1966).

[16] Roth v. United States, 354 U.S. 476 (1957).

[17] Memoirs v. Massachusetts (Fanny Hill), 383 U.S. 413, 418 (1966).

An argument like Lord Devlin's second argument can be constructed, and many of those who feel society is entitled to ban pornography are in fact moved by some such argument. It might take this form:

(1) If we permit obscene books freely to be sold, to be delivered as it were with the morning milk, the whole tone of the community will eventually change. That which is now thought filthy and vulgar in speech and dress, and in public behavior, will become acceptable. A public which could enjoy pornography legally would soon settle for nothing very much tamer, and all forms of popular culture would inevitably move closer to the salacious. We have seen these forces at work already—the same relaxations in our legal attitudes which enabled books like *Tropic of Cancer* to be published have already had an effect on what we find in movies and magazines, on beaches and on the city streets. Perhaps we must pay that price for what many critics plausibly consider works of art, but we need not pay what would be a far greater price for trash—mass-manufactured for profit only.

(2) It is not a sufficient answer to say that social practices will not change unless the majority willingly participates in the change. Social corruption works through media and forces quite beyond the control of the mass of the people, indeed quite beyond the control of any conscious design at all. Of course, pornography attracts while it repels, and at some point in the deterioration of community standards the majority will not object to further deterioration, but that is a mark of the corruption's success, not proof that there has been no corruption. It is precisely that possibility which makes it imperative that we enforce our standards while we still have them. This is an example—it is not the only one—of our wishing the law to protect us from ourselves.

(3) Banning pornography abridges the freedom of authors, publishers and would-be readers. But if what they want to do is immoral, we are entitled to protect ourselves at that cost. Thus we are presented with a moral issue: does one have a moral right to publish or to read "hard-core" pornography which can claim no value or virtue beyond its erotic effect? This moral issue should not be solved by fiat, nor by self-appointed ethical tutors, but by submission to the public. The public at present believes that hard-core pornography is immoral, that those who produce it are panderers, and that the protection of the community's sexual and related mores is sufficiently important to justify restricting their freedom.

But surely it is crucial to this argument, whatever else one might think of it, that the consensus described in the last sentence be a consensus of moral conviction. If it should turn out that the ordinary man's dislike of pornographers is a matter of taste, or an arbitrary stand, the argument would fail because these are not satisfactory reasons for abridging freedom.

It will strike many readers as paradoxical even to raise the question whether the average man's views on pornography are moral convictions. For most people the heart of morality is a sexual code, and if the ordinary man's views on fornication, adultery, sadism, exhibitionism and the other staples of pornography are not moral positions, it is hard to imagine any beliefs he is likely to have that are. But writing and reading about these adventures is not the same as performing in them, and one may be able to give reasons for condemning the practices (that they cause pain, or are sacrilegious, or insulting, or cause public annoyance) which do not extend to producing or savoring fantasies about them.

Those who claim a consensus of moral conviction on pornography must provide evidence that this exists. They must provide moral reasons or arguments which the average member of society might sincerely and consistently advance in the manner we have been describing. Perhaps this can be done, but it is no substitute simply to report that the ordinary man—within or without the jury box—turns his thumb down on the whole business.

A. R. Louch

Sins and Crimes

A law, say, prohibits homosexual conduct or punishes the prostitute for plying her trade. According to some it is a bad law, according to others a necessary one. Those who argue that it is a bad law do so on a variety of grounds—that it is sheer folly to try to change human nature by law, that such legislation can only be effective at the price of the right to privacy, that the punishment of acts arising from compelling desires is cruel and excessive, that the law has no business meddling in what people do to others with their consent. Those who argue that it is a necessary law do so on one ground, that the act in question is immoral, and that what is wrong must be punished, lest the law itself fall into disrepute by failing to carry out a consistent campaign against wrong-doing.

The issue might seem to be a simple one. There is a standard form of sexual expression, intercourse with a person to whom one is married. The question is as to whether the law should prohibit, ignore or condone other forms of sexual practice. The legal moralist, like James Stephen in the nineteenth century and Lord Devlin in our own, holds that unorthodox sexual conduct is manifestly wrong, and therefore must be an appropriate object for criminal legislation. Presumably then, his opponent, the libertarian, denies that unorthodox sexual acts are wrong, and so concludes that they are not appropriate objects for criminal legislation.

That, at least, comes close to Mill's attitude toward so-called moral offences, and he is surely the standard libertarian. For him, the mark of the immoral is also the mark of the criminal, for he seeks to devise a theory both of morals and of legislation that rests on facts, which he finds in the occurrence of intentionally inflicted injuries. Loss of life or limb, wounds or scars, empty safes and proofs of bankruptcy are undeniable

A. R. Louch is a professor of philosophy at Claremont Graduate School and chairman of the Department of Philosophy there. He is the author of articles in philosophy, and of *Explanation and Human Action* (2nd ed., 1969).

"Sins and Crimes" first appeared in *Philosophy*, Vol. 43 (1968), p. 163, and it is reprinted here by permission of the author and *Philosophy*.

occasions of harm, and their occurrence is susceptible of proof. Contrast such instances with feelings of embarrassment or indignation, annoyance or irritation, insult or shock and the point of Mill's criterion is made. These latter cases involve always an element of judgment, depending on differences of taste, legitimate differences in what people regard as important to them. They are inadequate bases for legislation since they leave too much to judgment; for Mill they are also inadequate grounds for determining what is moral and immoral, since morality too is to rest on a basis of unchallengeable facts. Thus consenting homosexuality, prostitution, and promiscuity escape the category of sin as well as that of crime. These acts are marked by consent and lack the signs of injury. Men and women knowingly and willingly engage in them and whether they are the worse for it is not something producible as a piece of evidence verifying a proposition or supporting an accusation in a court of law. Thus Mill's brand of libertarianism exempts consenting sexual conduct from legislative restraint because it fails the test of immorality, and not because he holds a thesis barring the influence of morality upon the law. Indeed, the paradigm case of an immoral act for Mill is the case also of a criminal act—deliberately doing something that causes palpable harm.

This view of Mill's, or my interpretation of it, is a useful way of applying pressure to other conceptions of the relation between crimes and sins, laws and morals. For example, the legal moralist could be asked to defend his view that sexual acts of various kinds are substantially immoral even though lacking the elements of coercion or deceit and palpable injury. He could thus be forced to produce, or to try to produce, an explication of morality instead of resorting to charges of immorality. More of this later. But it is especially useful as a way of accounting for the urge to raise up absolute legal barriers against legislation of certain kinds (e.g. moral legislation), an urge exhibited by many who fancy themselves good libertarians. Professor Hart is a good instance. He admits the charge of gross immorality levelled against the homosexual or the promiscuous, but wants nonetheless to exclude such acts from the reach of law. Now there is something compelling about the move from the charge of gross immorality to punishment. The legal moralist seems to be on strong ground in claiming that murder is punishable because wrong, and therefore that anything that is wrong is punishable. If it is admitted that the homosexual is engaged in grossly immoral acts, it is reasonable to suppose that the law could punish him for them.

To block this move, while admitting the immorality, Hart requires a principle of great power. He has to show that certain legal principles have a force that transcends the claim of sin.

It is to the credit of Hart and the many libertarians who take a line similar to his that they do such an effective job of presenting these restraining principles as absolutes. They point to two obstacles to legislative interference with private consenting acts that appear well-nigh insurmountable. The first has to do with the police work necessary to produce evidence that sexual vice has occurred. Since these crimes occur privately and with consent, methods of detection must almost certainly violate a man's privacy, by spying or resorting to trickery or fraud—e.g. by having an officer pose as a prostitute's client. Moreover, legislation against sexual vice is usually so vague that what counts as criminal wrong-doing is left to the judgment of the police officer. This may be due in part to the reticence of lawmakers to specify these crimes more exactly, since they are traditionally regarded as crimes not fit to be named. But even if the unmentionable should be mentioned it is not likely that legal specification serves the purpose intended. 'No one can see every way in which the wickedness of man may disrupt the order of society,' warns Lord Simonds, arguing in the *Shaw* case for discretionary power to law enforcers. But this is a warning to those who act as well as to those who enforce, for no one can see, either, what may appear criminally wicked to judges and policemen. There is simply something intrinsically vague and uncertain in laws directed against vice, and a danger that a man may be quite unaware that his actions are vicious in the eyes of the law.

Thus the whole attempt to use criminal law to supervise private, consenting acts jeopardises a man's right to privacy, deprives him of the possibility of knowing the precise nature of the charge against him, subjects him to *ex post facto* legislation, and licenses the police in the use of utterly nefarious investigative practices. Enough of a barrier, one might suppose, to provide an absolute limit to the scope of legislation.

If the main thrust of the libertarian argument is against vague legislation, the claim that morality is out of reach of the law is a much more modest thesis than it might otherwise appear to be. For what is at issue is whether law-enforcers should have the responsibility for determining whether an act is criminal, or whether this should always and without exception be determined by statute. This objection to the role of morals in law should not trouble the libertarian legislator, who would only be concerned to specify his immoral targets more exactly. The difference between the legal moralist and the libertarian would come down to their relative willingness or unwillingness to grant the police such discretionary powers. This, of course, is by no means a simple problem. Laws against traffic in obscenity are among the most vexing issues of this type, for obscenity is an area in which many people think some legislation is necessary, though they would agree that no guide-lines can possibly be spelled out in statute determining what counts as an obscene publication or performance. Thus such legislation is only possible if the police are granted discretionary power. The complete libertarian would, in such circumstances, give up the law; the complete legal moralist would not be troubled by police judgment. Most of us would probably fall in some indeterminate and unsatisfying position in between.

In any event, it is not clear that the main thrust of the libertarian argument is, or can be, directed wholly at vague laws. Moral offences can be perfectly clearly spelled out. Homosexuality, prostitution, fornication, adultery, fellatio, cunnilingus, bestiality—the vocabulary is both rich and definite, and laws exist on many a statute book prohibiting each and every one of these practices, and more besides. It is these quite definite acts that Hart wishes to exempt from legislative restraint, while admitting that they are substantially immoral. Hart and Devlin appear to be at loggerheads just because of their agreement that the act whose legal status they dispute is immoral. Hart says: right to undisturbed performance of private consenting acts is more important than the immorality of the act. Devlin says: 'When the help of the law is invoked by an injured citizen, privacy must be irrelevant' (p. 19). Is there any way a rational choice could be made between these claims, except to assert dogmatically either the absolute right to individual freedom or the absolute duty to punish immorality?

II

It is perhaps best to begin with the rhetoric by which Devlin manages to convince Hart that a good many private, consenting acts are vicious, even though he does not persuade him that all vicious acts should be punished.

In a way, of course, Devlin's remark, quoted above, is a piece of equivocation, borrowing the strong sense of injury from Mill and using it in the much weaker context in which injury is not shown, but alleged. It also overlooks the fact that in private consenting acts the injured citizen invoking the law's aid is not the person towards whom the act is directed and with whom it is performed. Devlin's injured citizen is the morally zealous bystander, offended at what other people do together to their mutual satisfaction. Devlin's remark makes it appear that the libertarian is denying the law's right to arrest a man for harming another in the privacy of his home. But the accent is not on privacy, but on consent, and on the absence of palpable marks of injury. Moreover, that the actions are done discreetly may seem to answer the complaint of the injured bystander. No one was setting out to offend *him*. He must have gone a bit out of his own way to suffer outrage, or even worse, his complaints must be based on his own too vivid imagination. To allow this man's complaints to require invasion of privacy is to expose the law to just those pressures Mill most feared, the intemperate and hypersensitive outcries of moral zealots. It is this fear especially that leads Mill to seek a narrow definition of crime that would deny to moral fanatics the extra force of police power in pursuing their designs against minority beliefs and practices. But Devlin, and the typical legal moralist, seem prepared to bow to the vociferous, misinterpreting it as the numerous, voice.

Still, the complaint of the moral zealot is not the whole story. Devlin is simply convinced that sexual aberrations are monstrous sins. By painting them in the most lurid colours he is able to put the maximum pressure on legal principles designed to restrain the law from punishing men for such acts. No wonder that his papers often contain passages that seem more appropriate to the ordinary man and the member of parliament than to the jurist. For in place of showing injury he must excite in his readers the emotions of fear and revulsion by harping on the corrupting power of sexual vice, as if succumbing to such temptations makes it impossible for a man to be honest, dependable, or brave. The technique is no doubt a rhetorical success, but it rests on a factual claim that is nowhere supported by evidence and probably cannot be. For this reason it may be ignored.

Devlin himself is not too pleased with his vivid pictures of sexual corruption, and turns to other means of establishing the immorality of homosexuality and licentiousness. Chief among these is the argument that sexual passion clouds judgment, and that a man at its mercy is not in a position to foresee the harm he may cause or the misery he must endure, once having succumbed to temptation. The law must protect him because he cannot be expected to protect himself.

There are analogies, of course, that nourish this paternalistic conviction. The law protects men (though it shouldn't, according to Mill) against possible sources of harm, where they are not in a position to make a judgment as to potential injury. Laws regarding the manufacture and sale of food and drugs, for example, rest on the twin suppositions that men are vulnerable, through ignorance that must characterise all but specialists, to various sources of impurity, and that these impurities cause demonstrable harm or constitute demonstrable deceit. The legal moralist must show that both these criteria are met in the sexual case, by drawing (perhaps) a convincing picture of men enticing women or boys by wile and deceit into practices that only ruin them. The law must protect the vulnerable against such scoundrels.

Unfortunately, it is not that easy to show demonstrable harm, and this is the fact that Mill harped on in the first place. The legal moralist, in fact, generally appeals to miseries that seem to be rather regular consequences of most human actions. If, on the other hand, he supports his case by appeal to the testimony of victims, he has to be rather selective, for the results of succumbing to temptation surely run all the way from misery and regret to joy and the discovery of happiness.

The moralistic argument is persuasive so long as it is clouded judgment that is stressed. This makes it appear as if law is required to prevent the meeting of opportunity and craving, for a mind disturbed by passion is incapable of judgment. Still, the other requisite of protective legislation is missing. It is not shown that injury is generally suffered as a result of failure of judgment. Other cases, like drug addiction, smoking or drinking to excess, serve the paternalist better just because the injurious consequences appear to be more nearly demonstrable. But in these cases it is difficult to show that clouded judgment prevents men from knowing the potential harm in advance. Indeed, as the fact of injury becomes increasingly uncontestable, the claim that men are incapable of making judgments as to injurious consequences becomes increasingly implausible. The paternalist is thus likely to overstate the danger or underestimate the capacity to judge. The first error saddles us with an excessive burden of legislation, the second opens the door to a situation in which the law so restricts choice that men have no alternative but to be upright.

III

Now these arguments of the legal moralist appear so easy to counter as to leave us no option but to endorse the libertarian position. This, however, is because the legal moralist fails to establish immorality, not because the libertarian has established privacy and consent as absolute restraints upon the law. To do this the libertarian would have to test these principles against a more readily admitted or established evil.

Consider the case of consenting violence. If a man hires me to kill him, am I guilty of murder in carrying out his instructions? If two men agree to settle their differences by a duel, and one falls, is the other guilty of murder? Of course, attitudes toward killing with consent differ from culture to culture. On the whole modern western law frowns upon it, and this is a tradition to which both legal moralists and libertarians subscribe. According to Anglo-American legal tradition, at least, violence *as such* is criminal; consent has nothing to do with it.

Some crimes, of course, require lack of consent for their performance. Stealing with consent in unintelligible; it is a bizarre form of giving. And this, perhaps, lends credence to the view that lack of consent is part of the definition of a criminal act. But the meaning of killing does not depend on lack of consent. A particular society may condone duelling, or rituals involving willing victims of human sacrifice, and in such a society where only the unwilling count as murdered, lack of consent may well be the sole criterion for crime. In a society prohibiting duelling or other voluntary acts of maiming and killing (even tattooing) it is clear that physical injury suffices to class an act as criminal.

It is, I suppose, our attitude toward violence—that it is wrong and inconsistent with our conception of a decent life—that leads us to override the fact of consent in prohibiting duelling, human sacrifice or Russian roulette. Violence threatens society by encouraging attitudes inimical to peace and security. These observations, it may be noted in passing, incorporate morality into the law. But what is of interest here is that these observations are exactly the sort that men like Devlin offer with regard to the sexual case. These acts, too, threaten society with disaster. Sexual preoccupations, and also those involving drugs, alcohol or gambling, turn men away from the duties and activities that keep society going. Furthermore, sexual interests outside the bonds of matrimony threaten the order of the family on which society is based. Thus it might be claimed that society has every right to protect itself against such potential threats, even if this means legislating in a way that overrides consent or guarantees of privacy.

And yet it is not homosexual, promiscuous or orgiastic desires in themselves that appear to shake society to its foundations. It is the thought that everyone will follow the minority down these garden paths. When men like Devlin see these practices as evidence of moral decay they are imagining what a social or moral order might be like in which everyone were homosexual, or where most men constantly pursued the ladies, abandoned themselves to the card table, or withdrew into alcoholic dreams or psychedelic fantasies. So long as these are minority pursuits society can assimilate them, and the law need not concern itself. The sexual desires of men are, perhaps, uniform enough and the natural tendency of men to bow to social disapproval strong enough, to keep potentially disruptive sexual variations in a manageable minority. When such natural governors are in operation, privacy and consent have their day. The danger caused to society by the undue sexual preoccupations of a minority must seem much less serious than an extension of police power or inroads upon privacy. The danger exists when these preoccupations are no longer those of a relatively stable minority, but show signs of increase, and so of becoming a way of life. This, Devlin rightly argues, cannot be. Such practices must continue to be the pastimes of the few if society is to continue to exist.

But then the moralist finds himself in the following dilemma. If, in the main, social practice reflects social ideals, laws enforcing these ideals are unnecessary; if it does not, legal means of ensuring performance consonant with these ideals are impractical, for they are no longer the effective ideals of the community. This suggests that the proposed analogue between violent acts and sexual acts is inexact. Violence and deceit might well be regarded as incompatible with *any* form of social organisation, sexual aberrations only with a *certain* set of mores. The moralist has been perturbed by changes he sees in the attitudes of the sexes toward one another and toward sexual cravings generally. These changes may threaten society with collapse—who knows? But they may only amount to that kind of change, at first hard to live with, especially for those who have grown up in different traditions, that signify not the end of society but only its transformation. A choice between these large-scale hypotheses seems quite beyond reach of judgment. And so, once again, the principles of privacy and consent flourish, not because they are absolutes but because the arguments or the evidence that might persuade us to override them are simply not convincing.

Hart himself, though admitting to the gross immorality and thus, by implication, the social threat, of departures from sexual custom, betrays his scepticism of that very claim. For in an argument that appears fundamental to his thesis, he claims that to punish sexual offences is to punish men for their desires, and that this is persecutory in effect. It is natural to wonder why preventing men from or punishing them for their sexual appetites should be regarded as cruel punishment when it never crosses the libertarian's mind that restraints upon the murderer or thief are also restraints upon his desires. It is no answer to appeal to strength of desire alone, for it must be as legitimate to suppose that murderers and thieves are compelled by desires beyond their control as it is to excuse sexual offenders on this ground. No, the answer seems rather to be found in the fact that sexual desires are looked upon at the start as somehow legitimate, a thing that no one will accord to acts of violence or deceit. This is not to applaud all sexual desires, of course, but only to admit that sexual desire has a legitimate role in human life, unlike lusts for blood or vengeance. Sexual passions are directed at times toward unusual objects or satisfied by unusual methods, and this strains the average man's capacity to let them pass without concern. But they are pleasurable pursuits to all concerned, and it is thus difficult to view them with the jaundiced eye that one casts upon violent actions.[1] This betrays, perhaps, a utilitarian bias, though it is important to notice the form it takes here. I am not arguing that pleasure is the good, or always good, nor any other form of that philosopher's dismemberment of the social views of Bentham. But I am arguing, with Mill, that pain, deliberately caused, is paradigmatic of what is bad, embodying, if you will, the definition of an immoral action, and serving at the same time as a criterion for a criminal offence. On this score there is ample reason to take the claim of gross immorality against sexual acts somewhat lightly. By the same token the right to privacy and the disbarring condition of consent loom large as ways of protecting sexual pastimes from

---

[1] Perhaps this leaves de Sade out of account. The result of that will be that I will be accused of not having *really* understood, or failed to plumb the depths, and so on. I should be inclined myself to think of sadism, whether in an obvious sexual form or not, as having primarily a violent, not a sexual character, at least for legal purposes. Thus legislation against it need not answer to the charge that the rights of private and legitimate desires are violated or consent ignored.

legal interference, the stature of these legal principles having been exaggerated by the puny claim of immorality against which they are placed.

In order to make the charge of gross immorality in sexual conduct stick, one must be convinced, as Devlin appears to be, that any form of sexual practice outside the bonds of matrimony (and no doubt many within it) threatens society to its foundations. Believing this, Devlin quite rightly rejects privacy and consent as boundaries to the law's reach. To argue with Devlin is thus, inevitably, to argue morally. There are no convenient legal expedients to which to retreat. The case of abortion illustrates this. It is sometimes argued that laws against abortion bring an illegitimate third party into the agreements between doctors and their patients. But this argument has force only so long as what the Catholic assumes is denied or ignored, that abortion is a case of taking life, and in fact a murderous case of it. Sooner or later this vexing question must be disposed of, if doctor-patient privacy is to be an issue at all.

By the same token the question, is non-orthodox sexual conduct vicious?, must sooner or later be faced, even though it involves deciding whether society as such is threatened, or only a particular and transitory form of social organisation and belief. It is easy to pay tribute to the difficulty of these questions by calling them sociological, making it appear that answering them is someone else's responsibility. The anthropologist, indeed, may provide instruction here, by describing the variety of sexual practices and attitudes from culture to culture. This may suggest the view that society is compatible with any form of sexual attitude. But the anthropologist also describes a wide variety of economic and social conditions within which sexual mores take shape. It may be that certain forms of sexual freedom are compatible with a relatively simple economic structure, but not with the complex urban industrial civilisation in which we happen to live. That society, we firmly believe, has witnessed the atrophy of all institutions capable of providing moral education and training for adult life save the immediate family. Noting this, Devlin might argue that sexual licence is indeed incompatible with society as we find it, whether or not totally different social forms can admit quite different sexual mores. Moreover, it is not within our power to abandon industry and flee the cities, Rousseau-like, so that we might allow the complete expression of human desires.

This is the power of Devlin's argument. The evil of deviant or excessive sexual practices is demonstrated in the threats they harbour to the very existence of society. Its weakness is simply that that threat is not proven. By the same token, the strength of the libertarian's argument is not in his appeal to immutable legal principles but quite simply in his challenge to the moral claim of his opponents. Indeed, in all these terribly solemn discussions of moral vice and legal principles it is forgotten to what extent attitudes toward sex allow for comic treatment, quite unlike murder, torture or the sadistic hinterland of the sexual. It is hard to maintain the view that departures from sexual orthodoxy threaten society while laughing at them at the theatre, in books, or at cocktail parties. The exaggerated moral claim simply does not ring true. For one thing the overwhelming temptations of sexual desire still appear to lead the vast majority of generation after generation into the depressingly normal outlets of marriage and family rearing. For another the results of departures from this normal pattern do not show unequivocal injury. For this reason, more than out of respect for inviolable legal principles, the case for the punishment of any consenting sexual acts, discreetly performed, must fail. And yet, of course, this conclusion leaves wide open the possibility that in some other case consent or privacy may not be adequate barriers to legislation.

IV

In any case the law-morals dichotomy will not help, for the libertarian view depends, if I am right, on taking a moral position counter to that advanced by the legal moralist. It may be worth speculating, in conclusion, on some of the reasons why this debate has come to be cast in the form of a law-morals dispute.

One reason has pretty clearly to do with the way in which morality comes to be identified with a rather particular brand of moral sentiment or a particular object of moral concern. At the crudest level morality is simply identified with sex, and prohibitions upon it, and thus the question as to whether morality is a proper sphere for law is the question whether sexual practices should be restrained by law. Not much more sophisticated is the tendency to abdicate morality to the morally ferocious, identifying it with the feelings of outrage, disgust or revulsion that some people feel toward the pleasures of others. Mill's insistence on the fact of injury is perhaps the best antidote to this peculiar, yet common, aberration.

On a more subtle level, much of the argument becomes entangled in the problem of punishment. Many people think that jails and work farms ought to be thought of as methods of rehabilitating or at worst ways of deterring men from their criminal habits, and thus suppose that they have divested themselves of old-fashioned 'moralistic' views of retribution. But this move, like that by which morality comes to be identified with the sexual or the intolerant, contains a covert assimilation of the concept of morality to the retributive attitude. And then of course a man who declares himself to be against morality in the law only means that he does not want law-breakers to be treated with vengeance. But the view he puts in its place, that law-breakers should be prevented from doing so again, or that they should be given therapy, clearly rests on the supposition that something is wrong that ought to be rectified or prevented. It is not clear to me why this is not a view as moral as that of the retributionist, nor how any legal action is possible at all unless it is animated by some conceptions of what is better or worse and what ought to be done and prevented.

A further subtlety has much to do with the Mill-Stephen and Hart-Devlin debates, where practices are at issue that some regard as good and desirable and others bad and revolting. The question is then as to whether those outraged should speak through law for society as a whole. The libertarian has the bad habit of abdicating morality to his opponent with the result that morality comes to be covertly identified with essentially contested (and vociferously expressed) opinions. No doubt the libertarian is right in rejecting the pressures of moral zealots on the law; but this is not because he has himself eschewed a moral view of the law. Murder is a crime because it is wrong, and wrong because of palpable injury. If consenting homosexuality is not a crime it is because it fails to exhibit the injuries that show murder or rape or theft to be both sins and crimes. To argue otherwise is to suppose that wrong-doing does not suffice to make an act criminal, forcing the libertarian to argue either that murder is criminal because of some non-moral quality, or that consent and privacy are together absolute barriers to the law. The second of these alternatives is highly dubious, the first, involving as it does the consequence that malicious injury is not morally wrong, little short of bizarre.

There are other and even more general ways in which the distinction between law and morals has been taken to have relevance to the question of sexual legislation. For example, as we have seen, much legislation of this sort depends for its enforcement on granting the police wide latitude in judging that an offence has been committed. The libertarian sometimes expresses his objection to this discretionary power by saying that law-enforcers should not make moral judgments. Perhaps this is extended to judges as well, in the hope that law-enforcers can be prevented from making law. This is no doubt a perfectly plausible if not always realisable hope, but it at most excludes morality from law *enforcement.* How law-*makers* are to decide what measures to support or oppose without recourse to ideas of what is good or bad is not recorded.

Nonetheless, most libertarians do seem to want a criterion for law-making that has the character of statute, thus eliminating moral judgment from the process of legislation. There are advantages in this. Just as the policeman can, in his work, appeal to something incontrovertible, the statute, so the legislator ought to be able to appeal to something equally incontrovertible, like natural law, or scientific facts, or basic norms. At this headwater of legal philosophy, the rejection of moral influence on the law, is the insistence that all justification must have the force that statutes have for the policeman. I think myself that the separation of law and morals is vitiated in this context by the incoherence of the demand. What appears to be wanted is that justification *within* the law (e.g. appeal to statute) shall apply also to justification *of* the law. Barring this, the legal positivist wishes to supplant appeal to principles with appeal to facts. Either alternative is self-defeating. Both ignore the necessity, in a novel situation, of making some judgment as to what sort of thing is regarded as good or bad, and thus worthy, by legal means, of facilitating or preventing. It is hard to see how the separation of law and morals at this level is anything more than a resolution to avoid thinking about law as an activity of human decision and judgment. But this is to avoid thinking about it as law.

So Hart, and many libertarians, in supposing that legislative restraint of sexual conduct should not be a matter of moral decision, appear to argue that the decision ought to rest on an appeal to statute. But the question all along is, should there be such statutes? And that question appears to depend on whether we are prepared to regard consenting sexual acts sinful enough to count as crimes.

Louis B. Schwartz

Morals Offenses and the Model Penal Code

What are the "offenses against morals"? One thinks first of the sexual offenses, adultery, fornication, sodomy, incest, and prostitution, and then, by easy extension, of such sex-related offenses as bigamy, abortion, open lewdness, and obscenity. But if one pauses to reflect on what sets these apart from offenses "against the person," or "against property," or "against public administration," it becomes evident that sexual offenses do not involve violation of moral principles in any peculiar sense. Virtually the entire penal code expresses the community's ideas of morality, or at least of the most egregious immoralities. To steal, to kill, to swear falsely in legal proceedings—these are certainly condemned as much by moral and religious as by secular standards. It also becomes evident that not all sexual behavior commonly condemned by prevailing American penal laws can be subsumed under universal moral precepts. This is certainly the case as to laws regulating contraception and abortion. But it is also true of such relatively uncontroversial (in the Western World) "morals" offenses as bigamy and polygamy; plural marriage arrangements approved by great religions of the majority of mankind can hardly be condemned out-of-hand as "immoralities."

What truly distinguishes the offenses commonly thought of as "against morals" is not their relation to morality but the absence of ordinary justification for punishment by a non-

Louis B. Schwartz is a professor of law at the University of Pennsylvania Law School. He is the author of *Free Enterprise and Economic Organization* (3rd ed., 1966) and a number of articles in the area of the criminal law. Professor Schwartz was co-author, with Professor Herbert Wechsler, of the *Model Penal Code of the American Law Institute* (1962).

"Morals Offenses and the Model Penal Code" was published in the *Columbia Law Review*, Vol. 63 (1963), p. 669, and is reprinted here by permission of the author and the *Columbia Law Review*.

theocratic state. The ordinary justification for secular penal controls is preservation of public order. The king's peace must not be disturbed, or, to put the matter in the language of our time, public security must be preserved. Individuals must be able to go about their lawful pursuits without fear of attack, plunder, or other harm. This is an interest that only organized law enforcement can effectively safeguard. If individuals had to protect themselves by restricting their movements to avoid dangerous persons or neighborhoods, or by restricting their investments for fear of violent dispossession, or by employing personal bodyguards and armed private police, the economy would suffer, the body politic would be rent by conflict of private armies, and men would still walk in fear.

No such results impend from the commission of "morals offenses." One has only to stroll along certain streets in Amsterdam to see that prostitution may be permitted to flourish openly without impairing personal security, economic prosperity, or indeed the general moral tone of a most respected nation of the Western World. Tangible interests are not threatened by a neighbor's rash decision to marry two wives or (to vary the case for readers who may see this as economic suicide) by a lady's decision to be supported by two husbands, assuming that the arrangement is by agreement of all parties directly involved. An obscene show, the predilection of two deviate males for each other, or the marriage of first cousins— all these leave non-participants perfectly free to pursue their own goals without fear or obstacle. The same can be said of certain nonsexual offenses, which I shall accordingly treat in this paper as "morals offenses": cruelty to animals, desecration of a flag or other generally venerated symbol, and mistreatment of a human corpse. What the dominant lawmaking groups appear to be seeking by means of morals legislation is not security and freedom in their own affairs but restraint of conduct by others that is regarded as offensive.

Accordingly, Professor Louis Henkin has suggested[1] that morals legislation may contravene constitutional provisions

---

[1] See Henkin, *Morals and the Constitution: The Sin of Obscenity*, 63 Colum. L. Rev. 391 (1963), to which the present article is a companion piece. Controversy on the role of the state in the enforcement of morals has recently reached a new pitch of intensity. See Hart, *Law, Liberty, and Morality* (1963); Devlin, *The Enforcement of Morals* (1959); Devlin, *Law, Democracy, and Morality*, 110 U. Pa. L. Rev. 635 (1962). I shall not attempt to judge this debate, *cf.* Rostow, The Sovereign Prerogative 45–80 (1962), and I leave it to others to align the present essay with one or another of the sides. The recent controversy traverses much the same ground as was surveyed in the nineteenth century. See Mill, *On Liberty* (1859); Stephen, *Liberty, Equality, Fraternity* (1873).

designed to protect liberty, especially the liberty to do as one pleases without legal constraints based solely on religious beliefs. There is wisdom in his warning, and it is the purpose of this article to review in the light of that warning some of the Model Penal Code[2] sections that venture into the difficult area of morals legislation. Preliminarily, I offer some general observations on the point of view that necessarily governed the American Law Institute as a group of would-be lawmakers. We were sensitive, I hope, to the supreme value of individual liberty, but aware also that neither legislatures nor courts will soon accept a radical change in the boundary between permissible social controls and constitutionally protected nonconformity.

I. Considerations in Appraising Morals Legislation

The first proposition I would emphasize is that a statute appearing to express nothing but religious or moral ideas is often defensible on secular grounds.[3] Perhaps an unrestricted flow of obscenity *will* encourage illicit sexuality or violent assaults on women, as some proponents of the ban believe. Perhaps polygamy and polyandry as well as adultery are condemnable on Benthamite grounds. Perhaps tolerance of homosexuality *will* undermine the courage and discipline of our citizen militia, notwithstanding contrary indications drawn from the history of ancient Greece. The evidence is hopelessly inconclusive. Professor Henkin and I may believe that those who legislate morals are minding other people's business, not their own, but the great majority of people believe that the morals of "bad" people do, at least in the long run, threaten the security of the "good" people. Thus, *they* believe that it is their own business they are minding. And that belief is not demonstrably false, any more than it is demonstrably true. It is hard to deny people the right to legislate on the basis of their beliefs not demonstrably erroneous, especially if these beliefs are strongly held by a very large majority. The majority cannot be expected

[2] The Model Penal Code is hereinafter cited as MPC. Unless otherwise indicated, all citations are to the 1962 Official Draft.

[3] See McGowan v. Maryland, 366 U.S. 420 (1961). The Supreme Court upheld the constitutionality of a law requiring business establishments to close on Sunday, on the ground that such regulation serves the secular goal of providing a common day of rest and recreation, notwithstanding that the statute proscribed profanation of "the Lord's day."

to abandon a credo and its associated sensitivities, however irrational, in deference to a minority's skepticism.

The argument of the preceding paragraph does not mean that all laws designed to enforce morality are acceptable or constitutionally valid if enough people entertain a baseless belief in their social utility. The point is rather that recognizing irrational elements in the controversy over morals legislation, we ought to focus on other elements, about which rational debate and agreement are possible. For example, one can examine side effects of the effort to enforce morality by penal law. One can inquire whether enforcement will be so difficult that the offense will seldom be prosecuted and, therefore, risk of punishment will not in fact operate as a deterrent. One can ask whether the rare prosecutions for sexual derelictions are arbitrarily selected, or facilitate private blackmail or police discriminations more often than general compliance with legal norms. Are police forces, prosecution resources, and court time being wastefully diverted from the central insecurities of our metropolitan life—robbery, burglary, rape, assault, and governmental corruption?

A second proposition that must be considered in appraising morals legislation is that citizens may legitimately demand of the state protection of their psychological as well as their physical integrity. No one challenges this when the protection takes the form of penal laws guarding against fear caused by threat or menace. This is probably because these are regarded as incipient physical attacks. Criminal libel laws are clearly designed to protect against psychic pain;[4] so also are disorderly conduct laws insofar as they ban loud noises, offensive odors, and tumultuous behavior disturbing the peace. In fact, laws against murder, rape, arson, robbery, burglary, and other violent felonies afford not so much protection against direct attack—that can be done only by self-defense or by having a policeman on hand at the scene of the crime—as psychological security and comfort stemming from the knowledge that the probabilities of attack are lessened by the prospect of punishment and, perhaps, from the knowledge that an attacker will be condignly treated by society.

If, then, penal law frequently or typically protects us from psychic aggression, there is basis for the popular expectation

---

[4] The Model Penal Code does not make libel a criminal offense. But this decision rests upon a judgment that the penal law is not a useful or safe instrument for repressing defamation; by no means is it suggested that the hurt experienced by one who is libelled is an inappropriate concern of government. See MPC § 250.7, comment 2 (Tent. Draft No. 13, 1961).

that it will protect us also from blasphemy against a cherished religion, outrage to patriotic sentiments, blatant pornography, open lewdness affronting our sensibilities in the area of sexual mores, or stinging aspersions against race or nationality. Psychiatrists might tell us that the insecurities stirred by these psychic aggressions are deeper and more acute than those involved in crimes of physical violence. Physical violence is, after all, a phenomenon that occurs largely in the domain of the ego; we can rationally measure the danger and its likelihood, and our countermeasures can be proportioned to the threat. But who can measure the dark turbulences of the unconscious when sex, race, religion or patriotism (that extension of father-reverence) is the concern?

If unanimity of strongly held moral views is approached in a community, the rebel puts himself, as it were, outside the society when he arraigns himself against those views. Society owes a debt to martyrs, madmen, criminals, and professors who occasionally call into question its fundamental assumptions, but the community cannot be expected to make their first protests respectable or even tolerated by law. It is entirely understandable and in a sense proper that blasphemy should have been criminal in Puritan Massachusetts, and that cow slaughter in a Hindu state, hog-raising in a theocratic Jewish or Moslem state, or abortion in a ninety-nine per cent Catholic state should be criminal. I do not mean to suggest a particular percentage test of substantial unanimity. It is rather a matter of when an ancient and unquestioned tenet has become seriously debatable in a given community. This may happen when it is discovered that a substantial, although inarticulate, segment of the population has drifted away from the old belief. It may happen when smaller numbers of articulate opinion-makers launch an open attack on the old ethic. When this kind of a beach-head has been established in the hostile country of traditional faith, then, and only then, can we expect constitutional principles to restrain the fifty-one per cent majority from suppressing the public flouting of deeply held moral views.

Some may find in all this an encouragement or approval of excessive conservatism. Societies, it seems, are by this argument morally entitled to use force to hold back the development of new ways of thought. I do not mean it so. Rather, I see this tendency to enforce old moralities as an inherent characteristic of organized societies, and I refrain from making moral judgments on group behavior that I regard as inevitable. If I must make a moral judgment, it is in favor of the individual visionaries who are willing to pay the personal cost to challenge the old moral order. There is a morality in some law-breaking, even when we cannot condemn the law itself as immoral, for it enables conservative societies to begin the re-examination of even the most cherished principles.

Needless to say, recognizing the legitimacy of the demand for protection against psychic discomfort does not imply indiscriminate approval of laws intended to give such protection. Giving full recognition to that demand, we may still find that other considerations are the controlling ones. Can we satisfy the demand without impairing other vital interests? How can we protect religious feelings without "establishing" religion or impairing the free exercise of proselytizing faiths? How can we protect racial sensibilities without exacerbating race hatreds and erecting a government censorship of discussion?[5] How shall we prevent pain and disgust to many who are deeply offended by portrayal of sensuality without stultifying our artists and writers?

A third aspect of morals legislation that will enter into the calculations of the rational legislator is that some protection against offensive immorality may be achieved as a by-product of legislation that aims directly at something other than immorality. We may be uneasy about attempting to regulate private sexual behavior, but we will not be so hesitant in prohibiting the commercialization of vice. This is a lesser intrusion on freedom of choice in personal relations. It presents a more realistic target for police activity. And conceptually such regulation presents itself as a ban on a form of economic activity rather than a regulation of morals. It is not the least of the advantages of this approach that it preserves to some extent the communal disapproval of illicit sexuality, thus partially satisfying those who would really prefer outright regulation of morality. So also, we may be reluctant to penalize blasphemy or sacrilege, but feel compelled to penalize the mischievous or zealous blasphemer who purposely disrupts a religious meeting or procession with utterances designed to outrage the sensibilities of the group and thus provoke a riot.[6] Reasonable rules for the maintenance of public peace incidentally afford a measure of protection against offensive irreligion. Qualms about public "establishment" of religion must yield to the fact that the alternative would be to permit a kind of violent private interference with freedom to conduct religious ceremonies.

---

[5] See MPC § 250.7 & comments 1–4 (Tent. Draft No. 13, 1961) ("Fomenting Group Hatred"). The section was not included in the Official Draft of 1962.
[6] See MPC §§ 250.8, 250.3 & comment (Tent. Draft No. 13, 1961).

It remains to apply the foregoing analysis to selected provisions of the Model Penal Code.

II. The Model Penal Code Approach

A. Flagrant Affronts and Penalization of Private Immorality
The Model Penal Code does not penalize the sexual sins, fornication, adultery, sodomy or other illicit sexual activity not involving violence or imposition upon children, mental incom-
petents, wards, or other dependents. This decision to keep
penal law out of the area of private sexual relations approaches
Professor Henkin's suggestion that private morality be immune
from secular regulation. The Comments in Tentative Draft No. 4
declared:

> *The Code does not attempt to use the power of the state to
> enforce purely moral or religious standards. We deem it inap-
> propriate for the government to attempt to control behavior
> that has no substantial significance except as to the morality
> of the actor. Such matters are best left to religious, educational
> and other social influences. Apart from the question of consti-
> tutionality which might be raised against legislation avowedly
> commanding adherence to a particular religious or moral tenet,
> it must be recognized, as a practical matter, that in a hetero-
> geneous community such as ours, different individuals and
> groups have widely divergent views of the seriousness of vari-
> ous moral derelictions.*[7]

Although this passage expresses doubt as to the constitutionality of state regulation of morals, it does so in a context
of "widely divergent views of the seriousness of various moral
derelictions." Thus, it does not exclude the use of penal sanctions to protect a "moral consensus" against flagrant breach.
The Kinsey studies and others are cited to show that sexual
derelictions are widespread and that the incidence of sexual
dereliction varies among social groups. The Comments proceed to discuss various secular goals that might be served by
penalizing illicit sexual relations, such as promoting the sta-
bility of marriage, preventing illegitimacy and disease, or fore-
stalling private violence against seducers. The judgment is
made that there is no reliable basis for believing that penal

---

[7] MPC § 207.1, comment at 207 (Tent. Draft No. 4, 1955).

laws substantially contribute to these goals. Punishment of private vice is rejected on this ground as well as on grounds of difficulty of enforcement and the potential for blackmail and other abuse of rarely enforced criminal statutes.[8] The discussion with regard to homosexual offenses follows a similar course.[9]

The Code does, however, penalize "open lewdness"—"any lewd act which [the actor] . . . knows is likely to be observed by others who would be affronted or alarmed."[10] The idea that "flagrant affront to commonly held notions of morality" might have to be differentiated from other sorts of immorality appeared in the first discussions of the Institute's policy on sexual offenses, in connection with a draft that would have penalized "open and notorious" illicit relations.[11] Eventually, however, the decision was against establishing a penal offense in which guilt would depend on the level of gossip to which the moral transgression gave rise. Guilt under the open lewdness section turns on the likelihood that the lewd act itself will be observed by others who would be affronted.

Since the Code accepts the propriety of penalizing behavior that affects others only in flagrantly affronting commonly held notions of morality, the question arises whether such repression of offensive immorality need be confined to acts done in public where others may observe and be outraged. People may be deeply offended upon learning of private debauchery. The Code seems ready at times to protect against this type of "psychological assault," at other times not. Section 250.10 penalizes mistreatment of a corpse "in a way that [the actor] . . . knows would outrage ordinary family sensibilities," although the actor may have taken every precaution for secrecy. Section 250.11 penalizes cruel treatment of an animal in private as well as in public. On the other hand, desecration of the national flag or other object of public veneration, an of-

---

[8] MPC § 207.1, comment at 205–10 (Tent. Draft No. 4, 1955).

[9] MPC § 207.5, comment at 278–79 (Tent. Draft No. 4, 1955). "No harm to the secular interests of the community is involved in atypical sex practice in private between consenting adult partners. This area of private morals is the distinctive concern of spiritual authorities. . . . [T]here is the fundamental question of the protection to which every individual is entitled against state interference in his personal affairs when he is not hurting others." MPC § 207.5, comment at 277–78 (Tent. Draft No. 4, 1955).

[10] MPC § 251.1; cf. MPC § 213.5, which penalizes exposure of the genitals for the purpose of arousing or gratifying sexual desire in circumstances likely to cause affront or alarm. This latter offense carries a heavier penalty than open lewdness, "since the behavior amounts to, or at least is often taken as, threatening sexual aggression." MPC § 213.4 & 251.1, comment at 82 (Tent. Draft No. 13, 1961).

[11] MPC § 207.1 & comment at 209 (Tent. Draft No. 4, 1955).

fense under section 250.9, is not committed unless others are
likely to "observe or discover." And solicitation of deviate
sexual relations is penalized only when the actor "loiters in or
near any public place" for the purpose of such solicitation.[12]
The Comments make it clear that the target of this legislation is
not private immorality but a kind of public "nuisance" caused
by congregation of homosexuals offensively flaunting their
deviance from general norms of behavior.[13]

As I search for the principle of discrimination between the
morals offenses made punishable only when committed openly
and those punishable even when committed in secrecy, I find
nothing but differences in the intensity of the aversion with
which the different kinds of behavior are regarded. It was the
intuition of the draftsman and his fellow lawmakers in the Institute that disrespectful behavior to a corpse and cruelty to
animals were more intolerable affronts to ordinary feelings
than disrespectful behavior to a flag. Therefore, in the former
cases, but not the latter, we overcame our general reluctance
to extend penal controls of immorality to private behavior that
disquiets people solely because they learn that things of this
sort are going on.

Other possible explanations do not satisfy me. For example,
it explains nothing to say that we wish to "protect" the corpse
or the mistreated dog, but not the flag itself. The legislation on
its face seeks to deter mistreatment of all three. All three cases
involve interests beyond, and merely represented by, the thing
that is immediately "protected." It is not the mistreated dog
who is the ultimate object of concern; his owner is entirely free
to kill him (though not "cruelly") without interference from
other dog owners. Our concern is for the feelings of other
human beings, a large proportion of whom, although accustomed to the slaughter of animals for food, readily identify
themselves with a tortured dog or horse and respond with
great sensitivity to its sufferings. The desire to protect a corpse
from degradation is not a deference to this remnant of a human
being—the dead have no legal rights and no legislative lobby
—but a protection of the feelings of the living. So also in the
case of the flag, our concern is not for the bright bit of cloth
but for what it symbolizes, a cluster of patriotic emotions. I
submit that legislative tolerance for private flag desecration is
explicable by the greater difficulty an ordinary man has in identifying with a country and all else that a flag symbolizes as

---

[12] MPC § 251.3; see text accompanying note 35 *infra*.
[13] MPC § 251.3, status note at 237.

compared with the ease in identifying with a corpse or a warm-blooded domestic animal. This is only an elaborate way of saying that he does not feel the first desecration as keenly as the others. Perhaps also, in the case of the flag, an element of tolerance is present for the right of political dissent when it goes no further than private disrespect for the symbol of authority.[14]

A penal code's treatment of private homosexual relations presents the crucial test of a legislator's views on whether a state may legitimately protect people from "psychological assault" by repressing not merely overt affront to consensus morals but also the most secret violation of that moral code. As is often wise in legislative affairs, the Model Penal Code avoids a clear issue of principle. The decision against penalizing deviate sexuality is rested not merely on the idea of immunity from regulation of private morality, but on a consideration of practical difficulties and evils in attempting to use the penal law in this way.[15] The Comments note that existing laws dealing with homosexual relations are nullified in practice, except in cases of violence, corruption of children, or public solicitation. Capricious selection of a few cases for prosecution, among millions of infractions, is unfair and chiefly benefits extortioners and seekers of private vengeance. The existence of the criminal law prevents some deviates from seeking psychiatric aid. Furthermore, the pursuit of homosexuals involves policemen in degrading entrapment practices, and diverts attention and effort that could be employed more usefully against the crimes of violent aggression, fraud, and government corruption, which are the overriding concerns of our metropolitan civilization.

If state legislators are not persuaded by such arguments to repeal the laws against private deviate sexual relations among adults, the constitutional issue will ultimately have to be faced by the courts. When that time comes, one of the important questions will be whether homosexuality is in fact the subject of a "consensus." If not, that is, if a substantial body of public opinion regards homosexuals' private activity with indifference, or if homosexuals succeed in securing recognition as a considerable minority having otherwise "respectable" status, this

---

[14] Not all legislatures are so restrained. See, *e.g.*, Pa. Stat. Ann. tit. 18, § 4211 (1945) ("publicly or privately mutilates, defaces, defiles or tramples upon, or casts contempt either by words or act upon, any such flag"). Query as to the constitutionality of this effort to repress a private expression of political disaffection.

[15] MPC § 207.5, comment at 278–79 (Tent. Draft No. 4, 1955).

issue of private morality may soon be held to be beyond resolution by vote of fifty-one per cent of the legislators.[16] As to
the status of homosexuality in this country, it is significant that
the Supreme Court has reversed an obscenity conviction involving a magazine that was avowedly published by, for, and
about homosexuals and that carried on a ceaseless campaign
against the repressive laws.[17] The much smaller group of
American polygamists have yet to break out of the class of
idiosyncratic heretic-martyrs[18] by bidding for public approval
in the same group-conscious way.

B. The Obscenity Provisions   The obscenity provisions of
the Model Penal Code best illustrate the Code's preference
for an oblique approach to morals offenses, *i.e.*, the effort to
express the moral impulses of the community in a penal prohibition that is nevertheless pointed at and limited to something
else than sin. In this case the target is not the "sin of obscenity," but primarily a disapproved form of economic activity—
commercial exploitation of the widespread weakness for titil-
lation by pornography. This is apparent not only from the narrow definition of "obscene" in section 251.4 of the Code, but
even more from the narrow definition of the forbidden behavior; only sale, advertising, or public exhibition are forbidden, and noncommercial dissemination within a restricted
circle of personal associates is expressly exempt.[19]

Section 251.4 defines obscenity as material whose "predominant appeal is to prurient interest. . . ."[20] The emphasis
is on the "appeal" of the material, rather than on its "effect,"
an emphasis designed explicitly to reject prevailing definitions
of obscenity that stress the "effect."[21] This effect is traditionally identified as a tendency to cause "sexually impure and

---

[16] *Cf.* Robinson v. California, 371 U.S. 905 (1962) (invalidating statute that penalized addiction to narcotics).

[17] One, Inc. v. Oleson, 355 U.S. 371 (1958), *reversing* 241 F.2d 772 (9th Cir. 1957). On the "homosexual community" see Helmer, *New York's "Middle-class" Homosexuals,* Harper's, March 1963, p. 85 (evidencing current non-shocked attitude toward this minority group).

[18] See Cleveland v. United States, 329 U.S. 14 (1946); Reynolds v. United States, 98 U.S. 145 (1878).

[19] MPC § 251.4(2), (3).

[20] (1) *Obscene Defined.* Material is obscene if, considered as a whole, its predominant appeal is to prurient interest, that is, a shameful or morbid interest, in nudity, sex or excretion, and if in addition it goes substantially beyond customary limits of candor in describing or representing such mat-ters. Predominant appeal shall be judged with reference to ordinary adults unless it appears from the character of the material or the circumstances of its dissemination to be designed for children or other specially susceptible audience. . . . MPC § 251.4(1).

[21] See MPC § 207.10, comment 6 at 19, 29 (Tent. Draft No. 6, 1957) (§ 207.10 was subsequently renumbered § 251.4).

lustful thoughts" or to "corrupt or deprave."[22] The Comments on section 251.4 take the position that repression of sexual thoughts and desires is not a practicable or legitimate legislative goal. Too many instigations to sexual desire exist in a society like ours, which approves much eroticism in literature, movies, and advertising, to suppose that any conceivable repression of pornography would substantially diminish the volume of such impulses. Moreover, "thoughts and desires not manifested in overt antisocial behavior are generally regarded as the exclusive concern of the individual and his spiritual advisors."[23] The Comments, rejecting also the test of tendency to corrupt or deprave, point out that corruption or depravity are attributes of character inappropriate for secular punishment when they do not lead to misconduct, and there is a paucity of evidence linking obscenity to misbehavior.[24]

The meretricious "appeal" of a book or picture is essentially a question of the attractiveness of the merchandise from a certain point of view: what makes it sell. Thus, the prohibition of obscenity takes on an aspect of regulation of unfair business or competitive practices. Just as merchants may be prohibited from selling their wares by appeal to the public's weakness for gambling,[25] so they may be restrained from purveying books, movies, or other commercial exhibition by exploiting the well-nigh universal weakness for a look behind the curtain of modesty. This same philosophy of obscenity control is evidenced by the Code provision outlawing advertising appeals that attempt to sell material "whether or not obscene, by representing or suggesting that it is obscene."[26] Moreover, the requirement under section 251.4 that the material go "substantially beyond customary limits of candor" serves to exclude from criminality the sorts of appeal to eroticism that, being prevalent, can hardly give a particular purveyor a commercial advantage.

---

[22] See MPC § 207.10, comment 6 at 19 n.21, 21 (Tent. Draft No. 6, 1957).

[23] MPC § 207.10, comment 6 at 20 (Tent. Draft No. 6, 1957).

[24] MPC § 207.10, comment 6 at 22–28 (Tent. Draft No. 6, 1957).

[25] See FTC v. R. F. Keppel & Brother, 291 U.S. 304 (1934) (sale of penny candy by device of awarding prizes to lucky purchasers of some pieces). The opinion of the Court declares that Section 5 of the Federal Trade Commission Act, proscribing unfair methods of competition, "does not authorize regulation which has no purpose other than . . . censoring the morals of business men," *ibid.*, p. 313, but that the Commission may prevent exploitation of consumers by the enticement of gambling, as well as imposition upon competitors by use of a morally obnoxious selling appeal.

[26] MPC § 251.4(2)(e). Equivalent provisions appear in some state laws. *E.g.,* N.Y. Pen. Law § 1141. There is some doubt whether federal obscenity laws reach such advertising. See Manual Enterprises, Inc. v. Day, 370 U.S. 478. 491 (1962). *But* see United States v. Hornick, 229 F.2d 120, 121 (3d Cir. 1956).

It is important to recognize that material may predominantly "appeal" to prurient interest notwithstanding that ordinary adults may actually respond to the material with feelings of aversion or disgust. Section 251.4 explicitly encompasses material dealing with excretory functions as well as sex, which the customer is likely to find *both* repugnant and "shameful" and yet attractive in a morbid, compelling way. Not recognizing that material may be repellent and appealing at the same time, two distinguished commentators on the Code's obscenity provisions have criticized the "appeal" formula, asserting that "hard core pornography," concededly the main category we are trying to repress, has no appeal for "ordinary adults," who instead would be merely repelled by the material.[27] Common experience suggests the contrary. It is well known that policemen, lawyers, and judges involved in obscenity cases not infrequently regale their fellows with viewings of the criminal material. Moreover, a poll conducted by this author among his fellow law professors—"mature" and, for the present purposes, "ordinary" adults—evoked uniformly affirmative answers to the following question: "Would you look inside a book that you had been certainly informed has grossly obscene hard-core pornography if you were absolutely sure that no one else would ever learn that you had looked?" It is not an answer to this bit of amateur sociological research to say that people would look "out of curiosity." It is precisely such shameful curiosity to which "appeal" is made by the obscene, as the word "appeal" is used in section 251.4.

Lockhart and McClure, the two commentators referred to above, prefer a "variable obscenity" concept over the Institute's "constant obscenity" concept. Under the "constant obscenity" concept, material is normally judged by reference to "ordinary adults."[28] The "variable obscenity" concept always takes account of the nature of the contemplated audience; material would be obscene if it is "primarily directed to an audience of the sexually immature for the purpose of satisfying their craving for erotic fantasy."[29] The preference for "variable obscenity" rests not only on the mistaken view that hard-core pornography does not appeal to ordinary adults,

---

[27] See Lockhart & McClure, *Censorship of Obscenity: The Developing Constitutional Standards,* 45 *Minn. L. Rev.* 72–73 (1960).

[28] The Model Penal Code employs the "variable obscenity" concept in part, since § 251.4(1) provides that "appeal" shall be judged with reference to the susceptibilities of children or other specially susceptible audience when it appears that the material is designed for or directed to such an audience.

[29] Lockhart & McClure, *supra* note 27, at 79.

but also on the ground that this concept facilitates the accomplishment of several ancillary legislative goals, namely, exempting transactions in "obscene" materials by persons with scholarly, scientific, or other legitimate interests in the obscene and prohibiting the advertising of material "not intrinsically pornographic as if it were hard-core pornography."[30] The Code accomplishes these results by explicit exemption for justifiable transactions in the obscene and by specific prohibition of suggestive advertising.[31] This still seems to me the better way to draft a criminal statute.

The Code's exemption for justifiable dealing in obscene material provides a workable criterion of public gain in permitting defined categories of transactions. It requires no analysis of the psyche of customers to see whether they are sexually immature or given to unusual craving for erotic fantasy. It makes no impractical demand on the sophistication of policemen, magistrates, customs officers, or jurymen. The semantics of the variable obscenity concept assumes without basis that the Kinsey researchers were immune to the prurient appeal of the materials with which they worked.[32] Would it not be a safe psychiatric guess that some persons are drawn into research of this sort precisely to satisfy in a socially approved way the craving that Lockhart and McClure deplore? In any event, it seems a confusing distortion of language to say that a pornographic picture is not obscene as respects the blasé [sexually mature?] shopkeeper who stocks it, the policeman who confiscates it, or the Model Penal Code reporter who appraises it.

As for the prohibition against suggestive advertising, this is certainly handled more effectively by explicitly declaring the advertisement criminal without regard to the "obscene" character of the material advertised than by the circumlocution that an advertisement is itself to be regarded as obscene if it appeals to the cravings of the sexually immature. That kind of test will prove more than a little troublesome for the advertising departments of some respectable literary journals.

If the gist of section 251.4 is, as suggested above, commercial exploitation of the weakness for obscenity, the question arises whether the definition of the offense should not be

---

[30] *Ibid.*

[31] MPC § 251.4(2)(e), (3)(a).

[32] *Cf.* United States v. 31 Photographs, 156 F. Supp. 350 (S.D.N.Y. 1957), in which, absent a statutory exemption, the court was compelled to rely on variable obscenity in order to sanction import of obscene pictures by the [Kinsey] Institute for Sex Research.

formulated in terms of "pandering to an interest in obscenity," *i.e.,* "exploiting such an interest primarily for pecuniary gain. . . ."[33] This proposal, made by Professor Henry Hart, a member of the Criminal Law Advisory Committee, was rejected because of the indefiniteness of "exploiting . . . primarily for pecuniary gain," and because it would clearly authorize a bookseller, for example, to procure any sort of hard-core pornography upon the unsolicited order of a customer. "Exploiting . . . primarily for pecuniary gain" is not a formula apt for guiding either judicial interpretation or merchants' behavior. It is not clear what the prosecution would have to prove beyond sale of the objectionable item. Would advertising or an excessive profit convert sale into "exploitation"? Would the formula leave a bookseller free to enjoy a gradually expanding trade in obscenity so long as he kept his merchandise discreetly under the counter and let word-of-mouth publicize the availability of his tidbits? Despite these difficulties, it may well be that the Code section on obscenity has a constitutional infirmity of the sort that concerned Professor Henkin insofar as the section restricts the freedom of an adult to buy, and thus to read, whatever he pleases. This problem might be met by framing an appropriate exemption for such transactions to be added to those now set forth in subsection (3).

The rejection of the Hart "pandering" formulation highlights another aspect of section 251.4, namely, its applicability to a class of completely noncommercial transactions that could not conceivably be regarded as "pandering." This ban on certain noncommercial disseminations results from the fact that subsection (2) forbids every dissemination except those exempted by subsection (3), and subsection (3) exempts noncommercial dissemination only if it is limited to "personal associates of the actor." Thus, a general distribution or exhibition of obscenity is prohibited even though no one is making money from it: a zealot for sex education may not give away pamphlets at the schoolyard gates containing illustrations of people engaged in erotic practices; a rich homosexual may not use a billboard on Times Square to promulgate to the general populace the techniques and pleasures of sodomy. Plainly, this is not the economic regulation to which I have previously tried to assimilate the Code's anti-obscenity regulations. But equally, it is not merely sin-control of the sort that evoked Professor Henkin's constitutional doubts. Instead, the community is merely saying: "Sin, if you must, in private. Do not flaunt your immoralities

[33] MPC § 207.10(1) (Tent. Draft No. 6, 1957) (alternative).

where they will grieve and shock others. If we do not impose
our morals upon you, neither must you impose yours upon us,
undermining the restraints we seek to cultivate through family,
church, and school." The interest being protected is not, directly or exclusively, the souls of those who might be depraved
or corrupted by the obscenity, but the right of parents to shape
the moral notions of their children, and the right of the general
public not to be subjected to violent psychological affront.

C. Prostitution   The prostitution provisions of the Model
Penal Code, like the obscenity provisions, reflect the policy
of penalizing not sin but commercial exploitation of a human
weakness, or serious affront to public sensibilities. The salient
features of section 251.2 are as follows. Sexual activity is
penalized only when carried on as a business or for hire. The
section covers any form of sexual gratification. "Promoters"
of prostitution—*i.e.*, procurers, pimps, keepers of houses of
prostitution—are penalized more severely than the prostitutes.
The patron of the prostitute is subject to prosecution for a
"violation" only, that is, he may be fined but not jailed, and the
offense is, by definition, not a "crime." Dependents of a prostitute are not declared to be criminals by virtue of the fact that
they live off the proceeds of prostitution, as under many present laws, but the circumstance of being supported by a prostitute is made presumptive evidence that the person supported
is engaged in pimping or some other form of commercial exploitation of prostitution.

The main issues in the evolution of the Institute's position on
prostitution were, on the one hand, whether to penalize all
"promiscuous" intercourse even if not for hire or, on the other
hand, whether even intercourse for hire should be immune
from prosecution when it is carried on discreetly out of the
public view. Those who favored extending the criminal law to
promiscuous noncommercial sexuality did so on secular, not
moral, grounds. They pointed to the danger that promiscuous
amateurs would be carriers of venereal disease, and they
argued that law enforcement against hire-prostitution would
be facilitated if the law, proceeding on the basis that most
promiscuity is accompanied by hire, dispensed with proof of
actual hire. Others doubted the utility or propriety of the law's
intervening in private sexual relations on the basis of a vague
and moralistic judgment of promiscuity; and these doubts pre-
vailed.

It was more strenuously contended that the Model Penal
Code should, following the English pattern, penalize prostitution only when it manifests itself in annoying public solicita-

tion.[34] This position was defeated principally by the argument that "call-houses" were an important cog in the financial machine of the underworld, linked to narcotics peddling and other "rackets." I find more interesting and persuasive the parallel between this problem of the discreet exploitation of sex and the suggestion in the obscenity context that discreet sale of obscene books to patrons who request them might not constitute "pandering." Both distinctions present the difficulty of drawing an administrable line between aggressive merchandising and passive willingness to make profits by catering to a taste for spicy life or literature.

Other provisions of section 251.2 also demonstrate its basic orientation against undesirable commerce rather than sin. The grading of offenses under the section ranges from the classification of the patron's guilt as a noncriminal "violation," through the "petty misdemeanor" classification (thirty day maximum imprisonment) for the prostitute herself, and the "misdemeanor" classification (one year maximum) for minor participation in the promotion of prostitution, to the "third degree felony" classification (five year maximum) for owning or managing a prostitution business, bringing about an association between a prostitute and a house of prostitution, or recruiting persons into prostitution. Clearly, from the point of view of the sinfulness of illicit sexual relations, the patron's guilt is equal to that of the prostitute, but it is the seller rather than the sinful customer who is labelled a criminal. And the higher the rank in the selling organization, the graver the penalty—a significant departure from the normal assimilation of accessorial guilt to that of the principal offender. This emphasis on the businessman in sex is underscored by the fact that the higher penalties applicable to him do not depend on whether he is the instigator of the relationship; if a prostitute persuades someone to manage her illicit business or to accept her in a house of prostitution, it is he, not she, who incurs the higher penalty.

In one respect, the Code's provisions against illicit sexual activity depart from the regulation of commerce. Section 251.3 makes it a petty misdemeanor to loiter "in or near any public place for the purpose of soliciting or being solicited to engage in deviate sexual relations." This extension is explained as follows in the accompanying status note:

[T]*he main objective is to suppress the open flouting of prevailing moral standards as a sort of nuisance in public thorough-*

[34] See Street Offenses Act, 1959, 7 & 8 Eliz. 2, c. 57.

fares and parks. In the case of females, suppression of professionals is likely to accomplish that objective. In the case of males, there is a greater likelihood that non-professional homosexuals will congregate and behave in a manner grossly offensive to other users of public facilities.[35]

The situation is analogous to that of noncommercial dissemination of obscenity by billboard publication or indiscriminate gratuitous distribution of pornography. In a community in which assemblages of "available" women evoke the same degree of violent resentment as assemblages of homosexuals, it would be consistent with this analysis to make public loitering to solicit illicit heterosexual relations an offense regardless of proof of "hire." On the other hand, the legislator may well decide that even in such a community it is not worth risking the possibility of arbitrary police intrusion into dance halls, taverns, corner drug stores, and similar resorts of unattached adolescents, on suspicion that some of the girls are promiscuous, though not prostitutes in the hire sense.

III. The Code's Position on Abortion

In present day, heterogeneous, secular American society, the law of abortion operates in an area of fundamentally conflicting views of morality. Here is no question of imposing conformity to community consensus on a few heretics or visionaries, but of employing the machinery of the state to coerce some major groups in the population to conform to the ideals of others. It is not a question of restricting the freedom of a few eccentrics to avoid inflicting great psychic injury on the bulk of the population, but of restricting the freedom of scores of millions of citizens, having conflicting but equally respectable sensibilities, to be protected.

The principle features of section 230.3—"Abortion"—are as follows. The Code recognizes additional justifications beyond those in prevailing law, which condemns any abortion unless continued pregnancy threatens the life or health of the mother. The additional justifications in the Code are the substantial risk that the child will be born with grave physical or mental defect or the fact that the pregnancy resulted from rape, incest, or other felonious intercourse, including in the last category any pregnancy resulting from illicit intercourse with a girl under sixteen. Justifiable abortions may be performed only by

---

[35] See MPC § 251.3, status note at 237.

licensed physicians and, except in emergencies, only in a licensed hospital. A woman is not liable for aborting herself, or attempting to do so, during the first twenty-six weeks of pregnancy (the greater risk to the woman and the progression of the foetus toward viable humanity in more advanced pregnancy distinguish the situation from self-abortion during early pregnancy). Subsection (5) penalizes "pretended abortion," *i.e.*, it is made a felony to use abortion procedures on a woman who is not pregnant. Subsection (6) confines trade in abortifacients to professional channels of pharmacy and medicine. Subsection (7) makes it clear that the ban on abortion is not to apply to the new oral "contraceptives" notwithstanding that they technically function after conception, *i.e.*, after the egg cell has already been fertilized by the sperm.

The data and argument presented in the Comments[36] support a more radical revision of prevailing abortion law than is embodied in the text of section 230.3. In substance, the secular case against a severely restrictive law rests upon evidence that the demand for abortions is so widespread and insistent that forcing the satisfaction of this demand into illicit channels results in financial victimization and death for thousands of women. This demand is by no means confined to cases in which the mother's life or health is threatened or in which there is reason to anticipate a defective child, or to cases of pregnancy resulting from felonious intercourse. It has been said that " 'the vast majority of all abortions equalling 90 per cent occur among married pregnant women, especially those between 25 and 35 years of age who have had several children.' "[37] These women seek abortions when the financial resources of the family are so limited that they fear hardships to themselves and their other children if additional burdens are taken on. The prospective mother may have a job or professional career that she cannot or will not interrupt for a confinement. She may have been deserted by her husband, or he may be an alcoholic or otherwise incompetent or dependent. Abortion may be sought by an unmarried woman who has already had several illegitimate children, all of whom stand a good chance of being added to the rolls of delinquency. None of these situations is brought within the bounds of lawful abortion by section 230.3.

The Comments also express a view of the proper relation-

---

[36] MPC § 207.11, comment 1 (Tent. Draft No. 9, 1959).

[37] MPC § 207.11, comment 1 at 147 (Tent. Draft No. 9, 1959), quoting Taussig, *Abortion, Spontaneous and Induced*, 387–88 (1936).

ship of criminal law and morality which, if accepted, would have carried the liberalization of the abortion law well beyond the moderate expansion of justifications provided in the section:

> *The criminal law in this area cannot undertake or pretend to draw the line where religion or morals would draw it. Moral demands on human behavior can be higher than those of the criminal law precisely because violations of those higher standards do not carry the grave consequence of penal offenses. Moreover, moral standards in this area are in a state of flux, with wide disagreement among honest and responsible people. The range of opinion among reasonable men runs from deep religious conviction that any destruction of incipient human life, even to save the life of the mother, is murder, to the equally fervent belief that the failure to limit procreation is itself unconscionable and immoral if offspring are destined to be idiots, or bastards, or undernourished, maleducated rebels against society. For many people sexual intercourse divorced from the end of procreation is a sin; for multitudes of others it is one of the legitimate joys of living. Those who think in utilitarian terms on these matters can differ among themselves as widely as moralists. Voluntary limitation of population can be seen as national suicide in a world-wide competition for numerical superiority, while to others uncontrolled procreation appears equally suicidal as tending to aggravate the pressure of population on limited natural resources and so driving nations to mutually destructive wars. To use the criminal law against a substantial body of decent opinion, even if it be minority opinion, is contrary to our basic traditions. Accordingly, here as elsewhere, criminal punishment must be reserved for behavior that falls below standards generally agreed to by substantially the entire community.*[38]

Had the foregoing considerations been given free play in the drafting of the section on abortion, the Institute would have had to go at least as far as the Swedish and Danish legislation, which permits abortion, not only on the ground of danger to the life or health of the mother, but also "if, taking into account the living conditions of the woman and other factors, there is reason to believe that her physical or mental strength would be seriously impaired by the birth and care of the

[38] MPC § 207.11, comment 1 at 150–51 (Tent. Draft No. 9, 1959).

child."[39] Under this legislation, a board composed of physicians, lawyers, and sociologists passes upon the propriety of abortion in particular cases, and the range of considerations in effect permits justification on social grounds as well as on health and eugenic grounds.

The failure of section 230.3 to reflect completely the logic of the Comments is inadequately explained in a single sentence at the end of Comment 6 referring to the absence of any "body of experience with such a law [*i.e.*, of the Swedish type] in the context of American Society" on which to base recommendations for a model provision. "[T]he draft refrains from taking any position for or against [additional] justifications. . . ." It would, perhaps, have been more candid to say that most of those involved in drafting and reviewing the Model Penal Code felt that any effort to introduce additional justifications would be so offensive to Catholic opinion as to impair seriously the legislative prospects of the Code as a whole.

What the Code does in abortion law is to move moderately away from the strict position against interruption of pregnancy. Although its provisions may not be in conformity with natural or moral laws as seen by the Catholic Church, it may prove to be not utterly offensive to the substantial body of Catholic opinion that does not insist upon conforming secular legislation in every respect to the moral requirements of natural law. To other groups in the population, the Code's inhibitions on abortion still amount to a very substantial restriction of freedom. It is difficult to formulate a secular justification for this restriction, at least as applied to interruptions of pregnancy at an early stage, for reasons that are persuasive to a large proportion of the population. Professor Henkin's thesis as to the unconstitutionality of punishing private sin may well be tested here rather than in the field of obscenity, so long as obscenity control efforts are limited to restraints on commercialization and restraints on public violation of standards that command virtually universal adherence.

---

[39] Quoted from the Swedish statute as set forth in MPC § 207.11, appendix at 166 (Tent. Draft No. 9, 1959). Compare the Danish provisions, quoted in MPC § 207.11, appendix at 165 (Tent. Draft No. 9, 1959), which require serious danger to health, but direct that in appraising this danger account shall be taken not only of physical or mental disease, but also of "weakness" under the conditions under which the woman has to live.

Gerald Dworkin

Paternalism

Neither one person, nor any number of persons, is warranted in saying to another human creature of ripe years, that he shall not do with his life for his own benefit what he chooses to do with it. [*Mill*]

I do not want to go along with a volunteer basis. I think a fellow should be compelled to become better and not let him use his discretion whether he wants to get smarter, more healthy or more honest. [*General Hershey*]

I take as my starting point the "one very simple principle" proclaimed by Mill in *On Liberty* . . . "That principle is, that the sole end for which mankind are warranted, individually or collectively, in interfering with the liberty of action of any of their number, is self-protection. That the only purpose for which power can be rightfully exercised over any member of a civilized community, against his will, is to prevent harm to others. He cannot rightfully be compelled to do or forbear because it will be better for him to do so, because it will make him happier, because, in the opinion of others, to do so would be wise, or even right."

This principle is neither "one" nor "very simple." It is at least two principles; one asserting that self-protection or the prevention of harm to others is sometimes a sufficient warrant and the other claiming that the individual's own good is *never* a sufficient warrant for the exercise of compulsion either by the society as a whole or by its individual members. I assume that no one, with the possible exception of extreme pacifists or anarchists, questions the correctness of the first half of the principle. This essay is an examination of the negative claim

Gerald Dworkin is a professor of philosophy at Massachusetts Institute of Technology. He is the author of articles in philosophy as well as the editor (with Judith Jarvis Thompson) of *Ethics* (1969).

"Paternalism" was written for and presented at a conference on legal philosophy and the law of torts held in 1968. It has not been previously published and it appears here by permission of the author. All rights reserved.

embodied in Mill's principle—the objection to paternalistic interferences with a man's liberty.

I

By paternalism I shall understand roughly the interference with a person's liberty of action justified by reasons referring exclusively to the welfare, good, happiness, needs, interests or values of the person being coerced. One is always well-advised to illustrate one's definitions by examples but it is not easy to find "pure" examples of paternalistic interferences. For almost any piece of legislation is justified by several different kinds of reasons and even if historically a piece of legislation can be shown to have been introduced for purely paternalistic motives, it may be that advocates of the legislation with an anti-paternalistic outlook can find sufficient reasons justifying the legislation without appealing to the reasons which were originally adduced to support it. Thus, for example, it may be that the original legislation requiring motorcyclists to wear safety helmets was introduced for purely paternalistic reasons. But the Rhode Island Supreme Court recently upheld such legislation on the grounds that it was "not persuaded that the legislature is powerless to prohibit individuals from pursuing a course of conduct which could conceivably result in their becoming public charges," thus clearly introducing reasons of a quite different kind. Now I regard this decision as being based on reasoning of a very dubious nature but it illustrates the kind of problem one has in finding examples. The following is a list of the kinds of interferences I have in mind as being paternalistic.

II

1. *Laws requiring motorcyclists to wear safety helmets when operating their machines.*
2. *Laws forbidding persons from swimming at a public beach when lifeguards are not on duty.*
3. *Laws making suicide a criminal offense.*
4. *Laws making it illegal for women and children to work at certain types of jobs.*
5. *Laws regulating certain kinds of sexual conduct, e.g. homosexuality among consenting adults in private.*
6. *Laws regulating the use of certain drugs which may have*

harmful consequences to the user but do not lead to anti-social conduct.

7. *Laws requiring a license to engage in certain professions with those not receiving a license subject to fine or jail sentence if they do engage in the practice.*
8. *Laws compelling people to spend a specified fraction of their income on the purchase of retirement annuities (Social Security).*
9. *Laws forbidding various forms of gambling (often justified on the grounds that the poor are more likely to throw away their money on such activities than the rich who can afford to).*
10. *Laws regulating the maximum rates of interest for loans.*
11. *Laws against duelling.*

In addition to laws which attach criminal or civil penalties to certain kinds of action there are laws, rules, regulations, decrees which make it either difficult or impossible for people to carry out their plans and which are also justified on paternalistic grounds. Examples of this are:

1. *Laws regulating the types of contracts which will be upheld as valid by the courts, e.g. (an example of Mill's to which I shall return) no man may make a valid contract for perpetual involuntary servitude.*
2. *Not allowing assumption of risk as a defense to an action based on the violation of a safety statute.*
3. *Not allowing as a defense to a charge of murder or assault the consent of the victim.*
4. *Requiring members of certain religious sects to have compulsory blood transfusions. This is made possible by not allowing the patient to have recourse to civil suits for assault and battery and by means of injunctions.*
5. *Civil commitment procedures when these are specifically justified on the basis of preventing the person being committed from harming himself. The D.C. Hospitalization of the Mentally Ill Act provides for involuntary hospitalization of a person who "is mentally ill, and because of that illness, is likely to injure himself or others if allowed to remain at liberty." The term injure in this context applies to unintentional as well as intentional injuries.*

All of my examples are of existing restrictions on the liberty of individuals. Obviously one can think of interferences which have not yet been imposed. Thus one might ban the sale of cigarettes, or require that people wear safety-belts in automobiles (as opposed to merely having them installed), enforcing this by not allowing motorists to sue for injuries even when caused by other drivers if the motorist was not wearing a seatbelt at the time of the accident.

I shall not be concerned with activities which though defended on paternalistic grounds are not interferences with the liberty of persons, e.g. the giving of subsidies in kind rather than in cash on the grounds that the recipients would not spend the money on the goods which they really need, or not including a $1,000 deductible provision in a basic protection automobile insurance plan on the ground that the people who would elect it could least afford it. Nor shall I be concerned with measures such as "truth-in-advertising" acts and Pure Food and Drug legislation which are often attacked as paternalistic but which should not be considered so. In these cases all that is provided—it is true by the use of compulsion—is information which it is presumed that rational persons are interested in having in order to make wise decisions. There is no interference with the liberty of the consumer unless one wants to stretch a point beyond good sense and say that his liberty to apply for a loan without knowing the true rate of interest is diminished. It is true that sometimes there is sentiment for going further than providing information, for example when laws against usurious interest are passed preventing those who might wish to contract loans at high rates of interest from doing so, and these measures may correctly be considered paternalistic.

III

Bearing these examples in mind, let me return to a characterization of paternalism. I said earlier that I meant by the term, roughly, interference with a person's liberty for his own good. But, as some of the examples show, the class of persons whose good is involved is not always identical with the class of persons whose freedom is restricted. Thus, in the case of professional licensing it is the practitioner who is directly interfered with but it is the would-be patient whose interests are presumably being served. Not allowing the consent of the victim to be a defense to certain types of crime primarily affects the would-be aggressor but it is the interests of the willing victim that we are trying to protect. Sometimes a person may fall into both classes as would be the case if we banned the manufacture and sale of cigarettes and a given manufacturer happened to be a smoker as well.

Thus we may first divide paternalistic interferences into "pure" and "impure" cases. In "pure" paternalism the class of persons whose freedom is restricted is identical with the class of persons whose benefit is intended to be promoted by such restrictions. Examples: the making of suicide a crime, requiring passengers in automobiles to wear seat-belts, requiring a Christian Scientist to receive a blood transfusion. In the case of "impure" paternalism in trying to protect the welfare of a class of persons we find that the only way to do so will involve restricting the freedom of other persons besides those who are benefitted. Now it might be thought that there are no cases of "impure" paternalism since any such case could always be justified on nonpaternalistic grounds, i.e. in terms of preventing harm to others. Thus we might ban cigarette manufacturers from continuing to manufacture their product on the grounds that we are preventing them from causing illness to others in the same way that we prevent other manufacturers from releasing pollutants into the atmosphere, thereby causing danger to the members of the community. The difference is, however, that in the former but not the latter case the harm is of such a nature that it could be avoided by those individuals affected if they so chose. The incurring of the harm requires, so to speak, the active cooperation of the victim. It would be mistaken theoretically and hypocritical in practice to assert that our interference in such cases is just like our interference in standard cases of protecting others from harm. At the very least someone interfered with in this way can reply that no one is complaining about his activities. It may be that impure paternalism requires arguments or reasons of a stronger kind in order to be justified, since there are persons who are losing a portion of their liberty and they do not even have the solace of having it be done "in their own interest." Of course in some sense, if paternalistic justifications are ever correct, then we are protecting others, we are preventing some from injuring others, but it is important to see the differences between this and the standard case.

Paternalism then will always involve limitations on the liberty of some individuals in their own interest but it may also extend to interferences with the liberty of parties whose interests are not in question.

IV

Finally, by way of some more preliminary analysis, I want to distinguish paternalistic interference with liberty from a related type with which it is often confused. Consider, for example, legislation which forbids employees to work more than, say, 40 hours per week. It is sometimes argued that such legislation is paternalistic for if employees desired such a restriction on their hours of work they could agree among themselves to impose it voluntarily. But because they do not the society imposes its own conception of their best interests upon them by the use of coercion. Hence this is paternalism.

Now it may be that some legislation of this nature is, in fact, paternalistically motivated. I am not denying that. All I want to point out is that there is another possible way of justifying such measures which is not paternalistic in nature. It is not paternalistic because, as Mill puts it in a similar context, such measures are "required not to overrule the judgment of individuals respecting their own interest, but to give effect to that judgment: they being unable to give effect to it except by concert, which concert again cannot be effectual unless it receives validity and sanction from the law." (*Principles of Political Economy*).

The line of reasoning here is a familiar one first found in Hobbes and developed with great sophistication by contemporary economists in the last decade or so. There are restrictions which are in the interests of a class of persons taken collectively but are such that the immediate interest of each individual is furthered by his violating the rule when others adhere to it. In such cases the individuals involved may need the use of compulsion to give effect to their collective judgment of their own interest by guaranteeing each individual compliance by the others. In these cases compulsion is not used to achieve some benefit which is not recognized to be a benefit by those concerned, but rather because it is the only feasible means of achieving some benefit which *is* recognized as such by all concerned. This way of viewing matters provides us with another characterization of paternalism in general. Paternalism might be thought of as the use of coercion to achieve a good which is not recognized as such by those persons for whom the good is intended. Again while this formulation captures the heart of the matter—it is surely what Mill is objecting to in *On Liberty*—the matter is not always quite like that. For example, when we force motorcyclists to wear helmets we are trying to promote a good—the protection of the person from injury—which is surely recognized by most of the individuals concerned. It is not that a cyclist doesn't value his bodily integrity; rather, as a supporter of such legislation would put it, he either places, perhaps irrationally, another value or good (freedom from wearing a helmet) above that of physical well-being or, perhaps, while recognizing the danger in the abstract, he either does not fully appreciate it or he underestimates the likelihood of its occurring. But now we are approaching the question of possible justifications of paternalistic measures and the rest of this essay will be devoted to that question.

V

I shall begin for dialectical purposes by discussing Mill's objections to paternalism and then go on to discuss more positive proposals.

An initial feature that strikes one is the absolute nature of Mill's prohibitions against paternalism. It is so unlike the carefully qualified admonitions of Mill and his fellow Utilitarians on other moral issues. He speaks of self-protection as the *sole* end warranting coercion, of the individual's own goals as *never* being a sufficient warrant. Contrast this with his discussion of the prohibition against lying in *Utilitarianism*:

Yet that even this rule, sacred as it is, admits of possible exception, is acknowledged by all moralists, the chief of which is where the with-holding of some fact . . . would save an individual . . . from great and unmerited evil.

The same tentativeness is present when he deals with justice:

It is confessedly unjust to break faith with any one: to violate an engagement, either express or implied, or disappoint expectations raised by our own conduct, at least if we have raised these expectations knowingly and voluntarily. Like all the other obligations of justice already spoken of, this one is not regarded as absolute, but as capable of being overruled by a stronger obligation of justice on the other side.

This anomaly calls for some explanation. The structure of Mill's argument is as follows:

1. *Since restraint is an evil the burden of proof is on those who propose such restraint.*
2. *Since the conduct which is being considered is purely self-regarding, the normal appeal to the protection of the interests of others is not available.*
3. *Therefore we have to consider whether reasons involving reference to the individual's own good, happiness, welfare, or interests are sufficient to overcome the burden of justification.*
4. *We either cannot advance the interests of the individual by compulsion, or the attempt to do so involves evils which outweigh the good done.*
5. *Hence the promotion of the individual's own interests does not provide a sufficient warrant for the use of compulsion.*

Clearly the operative premise here is (4), and it is bolstered by claims about the status of the individual as judge and appraiser of his welfare, interests, needs, etc.:

With respect to his own feelings and circumstances, the most ordinary man or woman has means of knowledge immeasurably surpassing those that can be possessed by any one else.

He is the man most interested in his own well-being: the interest which any other person, except in cases of strong personal attachment, can have in it is trifling, compared to that which he himself has.

These claims are used to support the following generalizations concerning the utility of compulsion for paternalistic purposes.

The interferences of society to overrule his judgment and purposes in what only regards himself must be grounded on general presumptions; which may be altogether wrong, and even if right, are as likely as not to be misapplied to individual cases.

But the strongest of all the arguments against the interference of the public with purely personal conduct is that when it does interfere, the odds are that it interferes wrongly and in the wrong place.

All errors which the individual is likely to commit against ad-
vice and warning are far outweighed by the evil of allowing
others to constrain him to what they deem his good.

Performing the utilitarian calculation by balancing the advantages and disadvantages we find that: "Mankind are greater
gainers by suffering each other to live as seems good to themselves, than by compelling each other to live as seems good
to the rest." Ergo, (4).

This classical case of a utilitarian argument with all the
premises spelled out is not the only line of reasoning present
in Mill's discussion. There are asides, and more than asides,
which look quite different and I shall deal with them later. But
this is clearly the main channel of Mill's thought and it is one
which has been subjected to vigorous attack from the moment
it appeared—most often by fellow Utilitarians. The link that
they have usually seized on is, as Fitzjames Stephen put it in
Liberty, Equality, Fraternity, the absence of proof that the
"mass of adults are so well acquainted with their own interests
and so much disposed to pursue them that no compulsion or
restraint put upon them by any others for the purpose of promoting their interest can really promote them." Even so sympathetic a critic as H. L. A. Hart is forced to the conclusion
that:

In Chapter 5 of his essay [On Liberty] Mill carried his protests
against paternalism to lengths that may now appear to us as
fantastic . . . No doubt if we no longer sympathise with this
criticism this is due, in part, to a general decline in the belief
that individuals know their own interest best.

Mill endows the average individual with "too much of the
psychology of a middle-aged man whose desires are relatively
fixed, not liable to be artificially stimulated by external in-
fluences; who knows what he wants and what gives him satis-
faction or happiness; and who pursues these things when he
can."

Now it is interesting to note that Mill himself was aware of
some of the limitations on the doctrine that the individual is
the best judge of his own interests. In his discussion of government intervention in general (even where the intervention does
not interfere with liberty but provides alternative institutions to
those of the market) after making claims which are parallel to
those just discussed, e.g. "People understand their own busi-

ness and their own interests better, and care for them more, than the government does, or can be expected to do." He goes on to an intelligent discussion of the "very large and conspicuous exceptions" to the maxim that:

Most persons take a juster and more intelligent view of their own interest, and of the means of promoting it than can either be prescribed to them by a general enactment of the legislature, or pointed out in the particular case by a public functionary.

Thus there are things

of which the utility does not consist in ministering to inclinations, nor in serving the daily uses of life, and the want of which is least felt where the need is greatest. This is peculiarly true of those things which are chiefly useful as tending to raise the character of human beings. The uncultivated cannot be competent judges of cultivation. Those who most need to be made wiser and better, usually desire it least, and, if they desired it, would be incapable of finding the way to it by their own lights.

. . . A second exception to the doctrine that individuals are the best judges of their own interest, is when an individual attempts to decide irrevocably now what will be best for his interest at some future and distant time. The presumption in favor of individual judgment is only legitimate, where the judgment is grounded on actual, and especially on present, personal experience; not where it is formed antecedently to experience, and not suffered to be reversed even after experience has condemned it.

The upshot of these exceptions is that Mill does not declare that there should never be government interference with the economy but rather that

. . . in every instance, the burden of making out a strong case should be thrown not on those who resist but on those who recommend government interference. Letting alone, in short, should be the general practice: every departure from it, unless required by some great good, is a certain evil.

In short, we get a presumption, not an absolute prohibition. The question is why doesn't the argument against paternalism go the same way?

I suggest that the answer lies in seeing that in addition to a purely utilitarian argument Mill uses another as well. As a Utilitarian, Mill has to show, in Fitzjames Stephen's words, that: "Self-protection apart, no good object can be attained by any compulsion which is not in itself a greater evil than the absence of the object which the compulsion obtains." To show this is impossible; one reason being that it isn't true. Preventing a man from selling himself into slavery (a paternalistic measure which Mill himself accepts as legitimate), or from taking heroin, or from driving a car without wearing seat-belts may constitute a lesser evil than allowing him to do any of these things. A consistent Utilitarian can only argue against paternalism on the grounds that it (as a matter of fact) does not maximize the good. It is always a contingent question that may be refuted by the evidence. But there is also a non-contingent argument which runs through *On Liberty*. When Mill states that "there is a part of the life of every person who has come to years of discretion, within which the individuality of that person ought to reign uncontrolled either by any other person or by the public collectively," he is saying something about what it means to be a person, an autonomous agent. It is because coercing a person for his own good denies this status as an independent entity that Mill objects to it so strongly and in such absolute terms. To be able to choose is a good that is independent of the wisdom of what is chosen. A man's "mode of laying out his existence is the best, not because it is the best in itself, but because it is his own mode." It is the privilege and proper condition of a human being, arrived at the maturity of his faculties, to use and interpret experience in his own way.

As further evidence of this line of reasoning in Mill, consider the one exception to his prohibition against paternalism.

In this and most civilised countries, for example, an engagement by which a person should sell himself, or allow himself to be sold, as a slave, would be null and void; neither enforced by law nor by opinion. The ground for thus limiting his power of voluntarily disposing of his own lot in life, is apparent, and is very clearly seen in this extreme case. The reason for not interfering, unless for the sake of others, with a person's voluntary acts, is consideration for his liberty. His voluntary choice is evidence that what he so chooses is desirable, or at least endurable, to him, and his good is on the whole best provided for by allowing him to take his own means of pursuing it. But by selling himself for a slave, he abdicates his liberty; he fore-

goes any future use of it beyond that single act. He therefore defeats,·in his own case, the very purpose which is the justification of allowing him to dispose of himself. He is no longer free; but is thenceforth in a position which has no longer the presumption in its favour, that would be afforded by his voluntarily remaining in it. The principle of freedom cannot require that he should be free not to be free. It is not freedom to be allowed to alienate his freedom.

Now leaving aside the fudging on the meaning of freedom in the last line it is clear that part of this argument is incorrect. While it is true that *future* choices of the slave are not reasons for thinking that what he chooses then is desirable for him, what is at issue is limiting his immediate choice; and since this choice is made freely, the individual may be correct in thinking that his interests are best provided for by entering such a contract. But the main consideration for not allowing such a contract is the need to preserve the liberty of the person to make future choices. This gives us a principle—a very narrow one—by which to justify some paternalistic interferences. Paternalism is justified only to preserve a wider range of freedom for the individual in question. How far this principle could be extended, whether it can justify all the cases in which we are inclined upon reflection to think paternalistic measures justified, remains to be discussed. What I have tried to show so far is that there are two strains of argument in Mill —one a straight-forward Utilitarian mode of reasoning and one which relies not on the goods which free choice leads to but on the absolute value of the choice itself. The first cannot establish any absolute prohibition but at most a presumption and indeed a fairly weak one given some fairly plausible assumptions about human psychology; the second, while a stronger line of argument, seems to me to allow on its own grounds a wider range of paternalism than might be suspected. I turn now to a consideration of these matters.

VI

We might begin looking for principles governing the acceptable use of paternalistic power in cases where it is generally agreed that it is legitimate. Even Mill intends his principles to be applicable only to mature individuals, not those in what he calls "non-age." What is it that justifies us in interfering with children? The fact that they lack some of the emotional and cognitive capacities required in order to make fully rational decisions. It is an empirical question to just what extent children have an adequate conception of their own present and future interests but there is not much doubt that there are many deficiencies. For example, it is very difficult for a child to defer gratification for any considerable period of time. Given these deficiencies and given the very real and permanent dangers that may befall the child it becomes not only permissible but even a duty of the parent to restrict the child's freedom in various ways. There is however an important moral limitation on the exercise of such parental power which is provided by the notion of the child eventually coming to see the correctness of his parent's interventions. Parental paternalism may be thought of as a wager by the parent on the child's subsequent recognition of the wisdom of the restrictions. There is an emphasis on what could be called future-oriented consent—on what the child will come to welcome, rather than on what he does welcome.

The essence of this idea has been incorporated by idealist philosophers into various types of "real-will" theory as applied to fully adult persons. Extensions of paternalism are argued for by claiming that in various respects, chronologically mature individuals share the same deficiencies in knowledge, capacity to think rationally, and the ability to carry out decisions that children possess. Hence in interfering with such people we are in effect doing what they would do if they were fully rational. Hence we are not really opposing their will, hence we are not really interfering with their freedom. The dangers of this move have been sufficiently exposed by Berlin in his *Two Concepts of Freedom.* I see no gain in theoretical clarity nor in practical advantage in trying to pass over the real nature of the interferences with liberty that we impose on others. Still the basic notion of consent is important and seems to me the only acceptable way of trying to delimit an area of justified paternalism.

Let me start by considering a case where the consent is not hypothetical in nature. Under certain conditions it is rational for an individual to agree that others should force him to act in ways which, at the time of action, the individual may not see as desirable. If, for example, a man knows that he is subject to breaking his resolves when temptation is present, he may ask a friend to refuse to entertain his requests at some later stage.

A classical example is given in the Odyssey when Odysseus commands his men to tie him to the mast and refuse all future orders to be set free, because he knows the power of the

Sirens to enchant men with their songs. Here we are on relatively sound ground in later refusing Odysseus' request to be set free. He may even claim to have changed his mind but since it is *just* such changes that he wished to guard against we are entitled to ignore them.

A process analogous to this may take place on a social rather than individual basis. An electorate may mandate its representatives to pass legislation which when it comes time to "pay the price" may be unpalatable. I may believe that a tax increase is necessary to halt inflation though I may resent the lower pay check each month. However in both this case and that of Odysseus the measure to be enforced is specifically requested by the party involved and at some point in time there is genuine consent and agreement on the part of those persons whose liberty is infringed. Such is not the case for the paternalistic measures we have been speaking about. What must be involved here is not consent to specific measures but rather consent to a system of government, run by elected representatives, with an understanding that they may act to safeguard our interests in certain limited ways.

I suggest that since we are all aware of our irrational propensities, deficiencies in cognitive and emotional capacities, and avoidable and unavoidable ignorance it is rational and prudent for us to in effect take out "social insurance policies." We may argue for and against proposed paternalistic measures in terms of what fully rational individuals would accept as forms of protection. Now clearly, since the initial agreement is not about specific measures we are dealing with a more-or-less blank check and therefore there have to be carefully defined limits. What I am looking for are certain kinds of conditions which make it plausible to suppose that rational men could reach agreement to limit their liberty even when other men's interests are not affected.

Of course as in any kind of agreement schema there are great difficulties in deciding what rational individuals would or would not accept. Particularly in sensitive areas of personal liberty, there is always a danger of the dispute over agreement and rationality being a disguised version of evaluative and normative disagreement.

Let me suggest types of situations in which it seems plausible to suppose that fully rational individuals would agree to having paternalistic restrictions imposed upon them. It is reasonable to suppose that there are "goods" such as health which any person would want to have in order to pursue his own good—no matter how that good is conceived. This is an argument used in connection with compulsory education for children but it seems to me that it can be extended to other goods which have this character. Then one could agree that the attainment of such goods should be promoted even when not recognized to be such, at the moment, by the individuals concerned.

An immediate difficulty arises from the fact that men are always faced with competing goods and that there may be reasons why even a value such as health—or indeed life— may be over-ridden by competing values. Thus the problem with the Christian Scientist and blood transfusions. It may be more important for him to reject "impure substances" than to go on living. The difficult problem that must be faced is whether one can give sense to the notion of a person irrationally attaching weights to competing values.

Consider a person who knows the statistical data on the probability of being injured when not wearing seat-belts in an automobile and knows the types and gravity of the various injuries. He also insists that the inconvenience attached to fastening the belt every time he gets in and out of the car outweighs for him the possible risks to himself. I am inclined in this case to think that such a weighing is irrational. Given his life-plans, which we are assuming are those of the average person, his interests and commitments already undertaken, I think it is safe to predict that we can find inconsistencies in his calculations at some point. I am assuming that this is not a man who for some conscious or unconscious reasons is trying to injure himself nor is he a man who just likes to "live dangerously." I am assuming that he is like us in all the relevant respects but just puts an enormously high negative value on inconvenience—one which does not seem comprehensible or reasonable.

It is always possible, of course, to assimilate this person to creatures like myself. I, also, neglect to fasten my seat-belt and I concede such behavior is not rational but not because I weigh the inconvenience differently from those who fasten the belts. It is just that having made (roughly) the same calculation as everybody else I ignore it in my actions. [Note: a much better case of weakness of the will than those usually given in ethics texts.] A plausible explanation for this deplorable habit is that although I know in some intellectual sense what the probabilities and risks are I do not fully appreciate them in an emotionally genuine manner.

We have two distinct types of situation in which a man acts in a nonrational fashion. In one case he attaches incorrect weights to some of his values; in the other he neglects to act in accordance with his actual preferences and desires. Clearly there is a stronger and more persuasive argument for paternalism in the latter situation. Here we are really not—by assumption—imposing a good on another person. But why may we not extend our interference to what we might call evaluative delusions? After all, in the case of cognitive delusions we are prepared, often, to act against the expressed will of the person involved. If a man believes that when he jumps out the window he will float upwards—Robert Nozick's example—would not we detain him, forcibly if necessary? The reply will be that this man doesn't wish to be injured and if we could convince him that he is mistaken as to the consequences of his action he would not wish to perform the action. But part of what is involved in claiming that the man who doesn't fasten his seatbelts is attaching an incorrect weight to the inconvenience of fastening them is that if he were to be involved in an accident and severely injured he would look back and admit that the inconvenience wasn't as bad as all that. So there is a sense in which if I could convince him of the consequences of his action he also would not wish to continue his present course of action. Now the notion of consequences being used here is covering a lot of ground. In one case it's being used to indicate what will or can happen as a result of a course of action and in the other it's making a prediction about the future evaluation of the consequences—in the first sense—of a course of action. And whatever the difference between facts and values—whether it be hard and fast or soft and slow—we are genuinely more reluctant to consent to interferences where evaluative differences are the issue. Let me now consider another factor which comes into play in some of these situations which may make an important difference in our willingness to consent to paternalistic restrictions.

Some of the decisions we make are of such a character that they produce changes which are in one or another way irreversible. Situations are created in which it is difficult or impossible to return to anything like the initial stage at which the decision was made. In particular, some of these changes will make it impossible to continue to make reasoned choices in the future. I am thinking specifically of decisions which involve taking drugs that are physically or psychologically addictive and those which are destructive of one's mental and physical capacities.

I suggest we think of the imposition of paternalistic interferences in situations of this kind as being a kind of insurance policy which we take out against making decisions which are far-reaching, potentially dangerous and irreversible. Each of these factors is important. Clearly there are many decisions we make that are relatively irreversible. In deciding to learn to play chess I could predict in view of my general interest in games that some portion of my free time was going to be pre-empted and that it would not be easy to give up the game once I acquired a certain competence. But my whole life-style was not going to be jeopardized in an extreme manner. Further it might be argued that even with addictive drugs such as heroin one's normal life plans would not be seriously interfered with if an inexpensive and adequate supply were readily available. So this type of argument might have a much narrower scope than appears to be the case at first.

A second class of cases concerns decisions which are made under extreme psychological and sociological pressures. I am not thinking here of the making of the decision as being something one is pressured into—e.g. a good reason for making duelling illegal is that unless this is done many people might have to manifest their courage and integrity in ways in which they would rather not do so—but rather of decisions, such as that to commit suicide, which are usually made at a point where the individual is not thinking clearly and calmly about the nature of his decision. In addition, of course, this comes under the previous heading of all-too-irrevocable decisions. Now there are practical steps which a society could take if it wanted to decrease the possibility of suicide—for example not paying social security benefits to the survivors or, as religious institutions do, not allowing persons to be buried with the same status as natural deaths. I think we may count these as inter-ferences with the liberty of persons to attempt suicide and the question is whether they are justifiable.

Using my argument schema the question is whether rational individuals would consent to such limitations. I see no reason for them to consent to an absolute prohibition but I do think it is reasonable for them to agree to some kind of enforced wait-ing period. Since we are all aware of the possibility of tem-porary states, such as great fear or depression, that are inimical to the making of well-informed and rational decisions, it would be prudent for all of us if there were some kind of institutional arrangement whereby we were restrained from making a decision which is so irreversible. What this would be like in practice is difficult to envisage and it may be that if no practical arrangements were feasible we would have to con-clude that there should be no restriction at all on this kind of action. But we might have a "cooling off" period, in much the same way that we now require couples who file for divorce to go through a waiting period. Or, more far-fetched, we might imagine a Suicide Board composed of a psychologist and another member picked by the applicant. The Board would be required to meet and talk with the person proposing to take his life, though its approval would not be required.

A third class of decisions—these classes are not supposed to be disjoint—involves dangers which are either not sufficiently understood or appreciated correctly by the persons involved. Let me illustrate, using the example of cigarette smoking, a number of possible cases.

1. *A man may not know the facts—e.g. smoking between 1 and 2 packs a day shortens life expectancy 6.2 years, the costs and pain of the illness caused by smoking, etc.*
2. *A man may know the facts, wish to stop smoking, but not have the requisite will-power.*
3. *A man may know the facts but not have them play the correct role in his calculation because, say, he discounts the danger psychologically since it is remote in time and/or inflates the attractiveness of other consequences of his decision which he regards as beneficial.*

In case 1 what is called for is education, the posting of warnings, etc. In case 2 there is no theoretical problem. We are not imposing a good on someone who rejects it. We are simply using coercion to enable people to carry out their own goals. (Note: There obviously is a difficulty in that only a subclass of the individuals affected wish to be prevented from doing what they are doing.) In case 3 there is a sense in which we are imposing a good on someone in that given his current appraisal of the facts he doesn't wish to be restricted. But in another sense we are not imposing a good since what is being claimed—and what must be shown or at least argued for—is that an accurate accounting on his part would lead him to reject his current course of action. Now we all know that such cases exist, that we are prone to disregarding dangers that are only possibilities, that immediate pleasures are often magnified and distorted.

If in addition the dangers are severe and far-reaching, we could agree to allow the state a certain degree of power to intervene in such situations. The difficulty is in specifying in advance, even vaguely, the class of cases in which intervention will be legitimate.

A related difficulty is that of drawing a line so that it is not the case that all ultra-hazardous activities are ruled out, e.g. mountain-climbing, bull-fighting, sports-car racing, etc. There are some risks—even very great ones—which a person is entitled to take with his life.

A good deal depends on the nature of the deprivation—e.g. does it prevent the person from engaging in the activity completely or merely limit his participation—and how important to the nature of the activity is the absence of restriction when this is weighed against the role that the activity plays in the life of the person. In the case of automobile seat-belts, for example, the restriction is trivial in nature, interferes not at all with the use or enjoyment of the activity, and does, I am assuming, considerably reduce a high risk of serious injury. Whereas, for example, making mountain-climbing illegal completely prevents a person from engaging in an activity which may play an important role in his life and his conception of the person he is.

In general, the easiest cases to handle are those which can be argued about in the terms which Mill thought to be so important—a concern not just for the happiness or welfare, in some broad sense, of the individual but rather a concern for the autonomy and freedom of the person. I suggest that we would be most likely to consent to paternalism in those instances in which it preserves and enhances for the individual his ability to rationally consider and carry out his own decisions.

I have suggested in this essay a number of types of situations in which it seems plausible that rational men would agree to granting the legislative powers of a society the right to impose restrictions on what Mill calls "self-regarding" conduct. However, rational men knowing something about the resources of ignorance, ill-will and stupidity available to the law-makers of a society—a good case in point is the history of drug legislation in the United States—will be concerned to limit such intervention to a minimum. I suggest in closing two principles designed to achieve this end.

In all cases of paternalistic legislation there must be a heavy and clear burden of proof placed on the authorities to demonstrate the exact nature of the harmful effects (or beneficial consequences) to be avoided (or achieved) and the probability of their occurrence. The burden of proof here is twofold— what lawyers distinguish as the burden of going forward and the burden of persuasion. That the authorities have the burden of going forward means that it is up to them to raise the question and bring forward evidence of the evils to be avoided. Unlike the case of new drugs where the manufacturer must produce some evidence that the drug has been tested and found not harmful, no citizen has to show with respect to self-regarding conduct that it is not harmful or promotes his best interests. In addition the nature and cogency of the evidence for the harmfulness of the course of action must be set at a high level. To paraphrase a formulation of the burden of proof for criminal proceedings—better 10 men ruin themselves than one man be unjustly deprived of liberty.

Finally, I suggest a principle of the least restrictive alternative. If there is an alternative way of accomplishing the desired end without restricting liberty although it may involve great expense, inconvenience, etc., the society must adopt it.

Shaw v. Director of Public Prosecutions; 2 All English Reports 446; (1962) Appeal Cases 220

The defendant, Frederick Charles Shaw, was the publisher of a 28-page booklet entitled *The Ladies' Directory*. Most of the pages contained the names and addresses of women who were prostitutes, together with a number of photographs of nude female figures. The booklet made it plain that the women advertising in the booklet could be reached at the telephone numbers listed and that they were offering their services for sexual intercourse and, in some cases, for the practice of sexual perversions.

Shaw was indicted on the following three counts:

1. *Conspiracy to corrupt public morals. Particulars of Offence. . . . conspired with certain persons who inserted advertisements in issues of a magazine entitled Ladies' Directory numbered 7, 7 revised, 8, 9, 10 and a supplement thereto, and with certain other persons whose names are unknown, by means of the said magazine and the said advertisements to induce readers thereof to resort to the said advertisers for the purposes of fornication and of taking part in or witnessing other disgusting and immoral acts and exhibitions, with intent thereby to debauch and corrupt the morals as well of youth as of divers other liege subjects of Our Lady The Queen and to raise and create in their minds inordinate and lustful desires.*
2. *Living on the earnings of prostitution, contrary to section 30 of the Sexual Offences Act, 1956.*
3. *Publishing an obscene article, the Ladies' Directory, contrary to section 2 of the Obscene Publications Act, 1959.*

Shaw was convicted after a jury trial on all three counts and sentenced to nine months imprisonment. He appealed his conviction on all three counts to the Court of Criminal Appeal, and when he lost there he was permitted to appeal counts (1) and (2) to the House of Lords. The House of Lords affirmed both convictions by a vote of four to one.

The following is a portion of Viscount Simonds' opinion in support of an affirmation of the conviction under count (1).

Opinion by Viscount Simonds

. . . My Lords, as I have already said, the first count in the indictment is "conspiracy to corrupt public morals," and the particulars of offence will have sufficiently appeared. I am concerned only to assert what was vigorously denied by counsel for the appellant, that such an offence is known to the common law, and that it was open to the jury to find on the facts of this case that the appellant was guilty of such an offence. I must say categorically that, if it were not so, Her Majesty's courts would strangely have failed in their duty as servants and guardians of the common law. Need I say, my Lords, that I am no advocate of the right of the judges to create new criminal offences? I will repeat well-known words: "Amongst many other points of happiness and freedom which your Majesty's subjects have enjoyed there is none which they have accounted more dear and precious than this, to be guided and governed by certain rules of law which giveth both to the head and members that which of right belongeth to them and not by any arbitrary or uncertain form of government." These words are as true today as they were in the seventeenth century and command the allegiance of us all. But I am at a loss to understand how it can be said either that the law does not recognise a conspiracy to corrupt public morals or that, though there may not be an exact precedent for such a conspiracy as this case reveals, it does not fall fairly within the general words by which it is described. I do not propose to examine all the relevant authorities. That will be done by my noble and learned friend. The fallacy in the argument that was addressed to us lay in the attempt to exclude from the scope of general words acts well calculated to corrupt public morals just because they had not been committed or had not been brought to the notice of the court before. It is not thus that the common law has developed. We are perhaps more accustomed to hear this matter discussed upon the question whether such and such a transaction is contrary to public policy. At once the controversy arises. On the one hand it is said that it is not possible in the twentieth century for the court to create a new head of public policy, on the other it is said that this is but a new example of a well-established head. In the sphere of criminal law I entertain no doubt that there remains in the courts of law a residual power to enforce the supreme and fundamental purpose of the law, to conserve not only the safety and order but also the moral welfare of the State, and that it is their duty to guard it against attacks which may be the more insidious because they are novel and unprepared for. That is the broad head (call it public policy if you wish) within which the present indictment falls. It matters little what label is given to the offending act. To one of your Lordships it may appear an affront to public decency, to another considering that it may succeed in its obvious intention of provoking libidinous desires it will seem a corruption of public morals. Yet others may deem it aptly described as the creation of a public mischief or the undermining of moral conduct. The same act will not in all ages be regarded in the same way. The law must be related to the changing standards of life, not yielding to every shifting impulse of the popular will but having regard to fundamental assessments of human values and the purposes of society. Today a denial of the fundamental Christian doctrine, which in past centuries would have been regarded by the ecclesiastical courts as heresy and by the common law as blasphemy, will no longer be an offence if the decencies of controversy are observed. When Lord Mansfield, speaking long after the Star Chamber had been abolished, said[1] that the Court of King's Bench was the custos morum of the people and had the superintendency of offences contra bonos mores, he was asserting, as I now assert, that there is in that court a residual power, where no statute has yet intervened to supersede the common law, to superintend those offences which are prejudicial to the public welfare. Such occasions will be rare, for Parliament has not been slow to legislate when attention has been sufficiently aroused. But gaps remain and will always remain since no one can foresee every way in which the wickedness of man may disrupt the order of society. Let me take a single instance to which my noble and learned friend Lord Tucker refers. Let it be supposed that at

---

[1] *Rex* v. *Delaval* (1763) 3 Burr. 1434, 1438, 1439.

some future, perhaps early, date homosexual practices between adult consenting males are no longer a crime. Would it not be an offence if even without obscenity, such practices were publicly advocated and encouraged by pamphlet and advertisement? Or must we wait until Parliament finds time to deal with such conduct? I say, my Lords, that if the common law is powerless in such an event, then we should no longer do her reverence. But I say that her hand is still powerful and that it is for Her Majesty's judges to play the part which Lord Mansfield pointed out to them.

I have so far paid little regard to the fact that the charge here is of conspiracy. But, if I have correctly described the conduct of the appellant, it is an irresistible inference that a conspiracy between him and others to do such acts is indictable. It is irrelevant to this charge that section 2 (4) of the Obscene Publications Act, 1959, might bar proceedings against him if no conspiracy were alleged. It may be thought superfluous, where that Act can be invoked, to bring a charge also of conspiracy to corrupt public morals, but I can well understand the desirability of doing so where a doubt exists whether obscenity within the meaning of the Act can be proved.

I will say a final word upon an aspect of the case which was urged by counsel. No one doubts—and I have put it in the forefront of this opinion—that certainty is a most desirable attribute of the criminal and civil law alike. Nevertheless there are matters which must ultimately depend on the opinion of a jury. In the civil law I will take an example which comes perhaps nearest to the criminal law—the tort of negligence. It is for a jury to decide not only whether the defendant has committed the act complained of but whether in doing it he has fallen short of the standard of care which the circumstances require. Till their verdict is given it is uncertain what the law requires. The same branch of the civil law supplies another interesting analogy. For, though in the Factory Acts and the regulations made under them, the measure of care required of an employer is defined in the greatest detail, no one supposes that he may not be guilty of negligence in a manner unforeseen and unprovided for. That will be a matter for the jury to decide. There are still, as has recently been said, "unravished remnants of the common law."[2]

So in the case of a charge of conspiracy to corrupt public morals the uncertainty that necessarily arises from the vague-

[2] Lord Radcliffe, "The Law and its Compass," p. 53.

ness of general words can only be resolved by the opinion of twelve chosen men and women. I am content to leave it to them.

The appeal on both counts should, in my opinion, be dismissed.

People v. Cohen;
1 C.A. 3d 94;
81 Cal. Rptr. 503
(1969)

Opinion by Judge Alarcon

132 Paul Robert Cohen was charged in a complaint filed in the
Municipal Court with a violation of section 415 of the Penal
Code. The complaint alleges that the defendant "did wilfully
and unlawfully and maliciously disturb the peace and quiet of
the neighborhood of 110 North Grand and the peace and quiet
of this complainant and other persons then and there being
present, by then and there engaging in tumultuous and offensive conduct." Trial by jury was waived. The defendant was
found guilty, probation was denied and he was sentenced to 30
days in the county jail.

Facts

On April 26, 1968, the defendant was observed in the Los
Angeles County Courthouse in the corridor outside of Division
20 of the Municipal Court wearing a jacket bearing the words
"Fuck the Draft" which were plainly visible. There were women
and children present in the corridor. The defendant was arrested. The defendant testified that he wore the jacket knowing that the words were on the jacket as a means of informing
the public of the depth of his feelings against the Vietnam War
and the draft.

The defendant did not engage in, nor threaten to engage in,
nor did anyone as the result of his conduct in fact commit or
threaten to commit any act of violence. The defendant did not
make any loud or unusual noise, nor was there any evidence
that he uttered any sound prior to his arrest.

Question Presented

Is offensive conduct which is not also tumultuous punishable under Penal Code section 415?[1]

Penal Code section 415 makes punishable a disturbance of the peace or quiet of a neighborhood by tumultuous *or* offensive conduct. If this statute is interpreted literally, any conduct which is tumultuous but not "offensive" is a crime and any conduct which is offensive but not "tumultuous" is a crime.

The appellant argues that he cannot be guilty of the crime of breach of the peace since his conduct consisted of the use of words unaccompanied by violence or the threat of violence.

It is the appellant's contention that the offense of disturbance of the peace does not exist without actual or threatened violence or behavior which is *likely* to create a disturbance. We agree with this statement of the law. However, we reach a different conclusion in applying the law to the facts.

Breach of the peace and disturbing the peace are synonymous terms. Section 415, when enacted in 1872, was a codification of the existing common law crime of breach of the peace. Therefore, in resolving the novel question presented us we can look to the common law to assist us in assaying the legislative intent behind the use of the words "offensive conduct."

In *Cantwell* v. *Connecticut,* 310 U.S. 296 at page 308 [84 L.Ed. 1213, 1220, 60 S.Ct. 900, 128 A.L.R. 1352] the United States Supreme Court stated the common law succinctly: "The offense known as breach of the peace embraces a great variety of conduct destroying or *menacing* public order and tranquility. It includes not only violent acts but acts and words *likely* to produce violence in others." (Italics added.)

The Restatement, Second, Torts, section 116 contains this definition of the crime of breach of the peace: "A breach of

---

[1] Penal Code section 415 provides as follows: "Every person who maliciously and willfully disturbs the peace or quiet of any neighborhood or person, by loud or unusual noise, or by tumultuous or offensive conduct, or threatening, traducing, quarreling, challenging to fight, or fighting, or who, on the public streets of any unincorporated town, or upon the public highways in such unincorporated town, run any horse-race, either for a wager or for amusement, or fire any gun or pistol in such unincorporated town, or use any vulgar, profane, or indecent language within the presence or hearing of women or children, in a loud and boisterous manner, is guilty of a misdemeanor, and upon conviction by any court of competent jurisdiction shall be punished by fine not exceeding two hundred dollars, or by imprisonment in the county jail for not more than ninety days, or by both fine and imprisonment, or either, at the discretion of the court."

the peace is a public offense done by violence, or likely to
cause an immediate disturbance of public order."

In California our appellate courts have evolved the same
definition for the crime of disturbing the peace.

(1)   Any act or conduct which disturbs the peace and quiet
by inciting violence or which tends to provoke others to break
the peace constitutes disturbance of the peace (*People* v.
Anderson, 117 Cal. App. Supp. 763, 767 [1 P.2d 64]; 9 Cal.Jur.
2d §§ 17–18). "It is not necessary that any act have in itself
any element of violence in order to constitute a breach of the
peace." (*People* v. *Green,* 234 Cal.App.2d Supp. 871, 873
[44 Cal.Rptr. 438].)

(2)   We conclude from the foregoing authorities that if it can
be reasonably anticipated that certain conduct will cause
others to disturb the peace, wilfully and maliciously engaging
in such behavior constitutes a disturbance of the peace.

Thus, under section 415 a person who engages in offensive
behavior which has a tendency to provoke *others* to acts of
violence or to in turn disturb the peace and quiet is guilty
of disturbing the peace although his own conduct, while offensive, was not in itself violent.

(3)   In the matter before us the defendant deliberately wore
a jacket emblazoned with language which is clearly offensive
and below the "minimum standard of propriety and the accepted norm of public behavior" (*Goldberg* v. *Regents of the
University of California,* 248 Cal.App.2d 867, 880 [57 Cal.Rptr.
463]) at least when paraded through a courthouse corridor
containing women and children. The defendant's conduct
consisted of more than a quiet and peaceful assertion of his
convictions about the draft. He carefully chose the forum for
his views where his conduct would have an effective shock impact. The defendant's stated purpose was to force a con-
frontation with others as to his opinion of the draft. The expression he chose to display on his jacket is one which is not
used publicly to espouse a philosophy or a personal conviction. He was intent upon attracting the attention of others to
his views by the sheer vulgarity of his expression. He must
have been aware that his behavior would vex and annoy a
substantial portion of his unwilling "audience." His conduct
was, therefore, malicious under Penal Code section 7.[2]

---

[2] Penal Code section 7 provides in part as follows: ". . . The words
'malice' and 'maliciously' import a wish to vex, annoy, or injure another
person, or an intent to do a wrongful act, established either by proof or
presumption of law . . ."

It was certainly reasonably foreseeable that such conduct might cause others to rise up to commit a violent act against the person of the defendant or attempt to forceably remove his jacket. The fact that the police intervened and that the defendant was arrested before violence occurred does not make his conduct any the less provocative. We think it also a reasonable inference from the time and place of the defendant's act that he intended to provoke disorder.

It is our conclusion that the defendant's acts constituted the type of offensive conduct prohibited by section 415 in that it had a tendency to incite others to violent behavior or to disturb the peace.

(4) It is also our view that it is not a valid defense to a charge of disturbing the peace that the defendant's conduct was not violent or tumultuous if it was foreseeable that his acts would tend to cause others to commit violent acts or disturb the peace.

(5) The court minutes reflect that the defendant was found guilty as charged. The complaint charged him with engaging in tumultuous *and* offensive conduct. There was no evidence that the defendant engaged in "tumultuous" conduct. Penal Code section 415 sets forth a series of acts in the disjunctive. When an accusatory pleading sets forth more than one act prohibited by section 415 in the conjunctive, evidence which is sufficient to support a finding of guilt of any one of the acts denounced by the statute is sufficient for a conviction although the evidence does not support a conviction for each of the acts set out in the complaint (*People* v. *McClennegen,* 195 Cal. 445, 452 [234 P. 91]).

(6) The appellant also contends that the term "offensive" is unconstitutionally vague and overbroad. We disagree. In *People* v. *Green,* 234 Cal.App.2d Supp. 871, 875 [44 Cal.Rptr. 438] cert. denied, 382 U.S. 993 [15 L.Ed.2d 480, 86 S.Ct. 576], Penal Code section 415 was held to be "not unconstitutionally vague or indefinite." We feel the language relied upon by the California Supreme Court in *People* v. *Daniels* (October 2, 1969)[3] 71 Cal.2d ——, —— [—— Cal.Rptr. ——, —— P.2d ——] is particularly applicable as a standard in construing the constitutional scope of the term "offensive" as used in section 415. "In reaching this conclusion we invoked the settled rule of statutory interpretation that 'All laws should receive a sensible construction. General terms should be so limited in their

[3] Advance Report Citation: 71 A.C. 1165, 1176.

application as to not lead to injustice, oppression, or an absurd consequence. *It will always, therefore, be presumed that the Legislature intended exceptions to its language, which would avoid results of this character. The reason of the law in such cases should prevail over the letter.'"* (*United States* v. *Kirby* (1869) 74 U.S. (7 Wall) 482, 486–487 [19 L.Ed. 278, 280] accord; *People* v. *Oliver* (1961) 55 Cal.2d 761, 767 [21 Cal.Rptr. 865, 361 P.2d 593], and cases cited.) (Italics added.)

The words "offensive conduct" have stood the test of time and have a commonly accepted meaning. The term "offensive" has a well established meaning when used in connection with words which can cause a breach of the peace. In *Chaplinsky* v. *New Hampshire,* 315 U.S. 568, 571–572 [86 L.Ed. 1031, 1034–1035, 62 S.Ct. 766], the United States Supreme Court quoted with approval the following language from the opinion of the Supreme Court of New Hampshire in *State* v. *Chaplinsky,* 91 N.H. 310 [18 A.2d 754]: "The word 'offensive' is not to be defined in terms of what a particular addressee thinks. . . . The test is what men of common intelligence would understand would be words likely to cause an average addressee to fight. . . . The English language has a number of words and expressions which by general consent are 'fighting words' when said without a disarming smile. . . . Such words, as ordinary men know, are likely to cause a fight. So are threatening, profane or obscene revilings. Derisive and annoying words can be taken as coming within the purview of the statute as heretofore interpreted only when they have this characteristic of plainly tending to excite the addressee to a breach of the peace. . . . The statute, as construed, does no more than prohibit the face-to-face words plainly likely to cause a breach of the peace by the addressee, words whose speaking constitute a breach of the peace by the speaker—including 'classical fighting words,' words in current use less 'classical' but equally likely to cause violence, and other disorderly words, including profanity, obscenity and threats."

As modified by case law the only "offensive" conduct prohibited by section 415 is that which incites violence or has a tendency to incite others to violence or a breach of the peace. (Cf. *People* v. *Davis,* 68 Cal.2d 481, 486–487 [67 Cal.Rptr. 547, 439 P.2d 651].) This standard makes clear for triers of fact the nature of the forbidden conduct, and eliminates prosecutions or convictions for conduct which is merely offensive.

The appellant argues that Penal Code section 415 if interpreted to prohibit the behavior which led to his arrest and conviction violates his right to freedom of speech as guaranteed by the First Amendment.

In analyzing this constitutional attack we can look to the guidelines set forth in opinions of the United States Supreme Court involving the conflict created by the co-existence of the right of freedom of speech and the crime of disturbance of the peace where the alleged disturbance involves the use of language.

(7) Freedom of speech is not absolute. It must be balanced against other public interests (*American Communications Assn.* v. *Douds,* 339 U.S. 382, 399 [94 L.Ed. 925, 944, 70 S.Ct. 674]; *Breard* v. *Alexandria,* 341 U.S. 622, 642 [95 L.Ed. 1233, 1248, 71 S.Ct. 920, 35 A.L.R.3d 335]). ". . . when 'speech' and 'non-speech' elements are combined in the same course of conduct, a sufficiently important governmental interest in regulating the non-speech element can justify incidental limitations on First Amendment freedoms." (*United States* v. *O'Brien,* 391, 367, 376 [20 L.Ed.2d 672, 680, S.Ct. 1673].)

(8) The First Amendment does not afford any protection to one who uses language which tends to incite violence or a disturbance of the peace by others. "There are certain well-defined and narrowly limited classes of speech, the prevention and punishment of which have never been thought to raise any constitutional problem. These include the lewd and obscene, the profane, the libelous, and the insulting or 'fighting' words— those which by their very utterance inflict injury or tend to incite to an immediate breach of the peace. It has been well observed that such utterances are no essential part of any such exposition of ideas, and are of such slight social value as a step to truth that any benefit that may be derived from them is clearly outweighed by the social interest in order and morality. (9) 'Resort to epithets or personal abuse is not in any proper sense communication of information or opinion safeguarded by the Constitution, and its punishment as a criminal act would raise no question under that instrument.' *Cantwell* v. *Connecticut,* 310 U.S. 296, 309–310 [84 L.Ed. 1213, 1220–1221, 60 S.Ct. 900, 128 A.L.R. 1352]." (*Beauharnais* v. *Illinois,* 343 U.S. 250, 255 [96 L.Ed. 919, 926, 72 S.Ct. 725]; *Chaplinsky* v. *New Hampshire,* 315 U.S. 568, 571–572 [86 L.Ed. 1031, 1034–1035, 62 S.Ct. 766].)

(10) The right to freedom of speech does not protect illegal conduct merely because it is in part initiated, evidenced, or carried out by means of language either spoken, written, or printed. (*Giboney* v. *Empire Storage & Ice Co.,* 336 U.S. 490,

502 [93 L.Ed. 834, 843, 69 S.Ct. 684]; *Cox* v. *Louisiana,* 379 U.S.
559, 563 [13 L.Ed.2d 487, 491–492, 85 S.Ct. 476]; *People* v.
Davis, 68 Cal.2d 481, 486 [67 Cal.Rptr. 547, 439 P.2d 651].)

(11) "When protest takes the form of mass demonstration,
parades, or picketing on public streets and sidewalks, the free
passage of traffic and *the prevention of public disorder and
violence* become important objects of legitimate state concern.
As the court stated in *Cox* v. *Louisiana,* 'We emphatically reject
the notion . . . that the First and Fourteenth Amendments afford the same freedom to those who would communicate ideas
by conduct such as patroling, marching, and picketing on
streets and highways, as these amendments afford to those
who communicate ideas by pure speech, 379 U.S. 536, 555 [13
L.Ed.2d 471, 484, 85 S.Ct. 453].' " (Italics added.) (*Walker* v.
Birmingham, 338 U.S. 307, 316 [18 L.Ed.2d 1210, 1217, 87 S.Ct.
1824].)

"One may . . . be guilty of the offense [of breach of the
peace] if he commits acts or makes statements likely to provoke violence or disturbance of good order, even though no
such eventuality be intended." (*Cantwell* v. *Connecticut,* 310
U.S. 296, 396 [84 L.Ed. 1213, 1221, 60 S.Ct. 900, 128 A.L.R.
1352].)

(12) In the case before us, the defendant's conduct consisted of "speech" and "non-speech" elements. Here the non-
speech element of the defendant's conduct consisted of marching through a public building with the premeditated intent of
attracting the attention of others to the message on his jacket.

The gravaman of the defendant's offense was his selection
of the public corridors of the county courthouse as the place to
parade before women and children who were involuntarily subjected to unprintable language. The expression used by the
defendant to propagate his views is one of the most notorious
four-letter words in the English language. Despite its ancient
origins, it has yet to gain sufficient acceptance to appear in
any standard dictionary (cf. Webster's Third New International
Dictionary; The Oxford Dictionary of American English; The
Oxford English Dictionary). In the work "A Dictionary of Slang
and Unconventional English" by Eric Partridge, the word is
defined; however, the second letter has been replaced with an
asterisk.

The defendant has not been subjected to prosecution for
expressing his political views. His right to speak out against
the draft and war is protected by the First Amendment. However, no one has the right to express his views by means of
printing lewd and vulgar language which is likely to cause

others to breach the peace to protect women and children from such exposure.

It is our view, based on our interpretation of the decisions of the United States Supreme Court, that the defendant's conduct in this case went beyond the permissive ambit of the First Amendment's protection as circumscribed in the *Cantwell, supra, Chaplinsky, supra,* and *Beauharnais, supra,* cases.

(13) The trial judge ruled that although the complaint charged the defendant with disturbing the peace by means of tumultuous and offensive conduct, the defendant could be found guilty of the use of "vulgar, profane, or indecent language within the presence of or hearing of women or children in a loud boisterous manner," conduct also prohibited by section 415 of the Penal Code. This ruling was incorrect. Proof that the language was uttered in a "loud and boisterous" manner is "a very necessary matter to complete the offense" of disturbing the peace by the use of vulgar, profane and indecent language in the presence or hearing of women and children (*Ex parte Boynton,* 1 Cal.App. 294 [82 P. 90]). In the present case there was no proof that the defendant engaged in any loud or boisterous conduct. Furthermore, a person cannot be found guilty of a crime with which he was not charged. "Conviction upon a charge not made would be sheer denial of due process." (*De Jonge* v. *Oregon,* 299 U.S. 353, 362 [81 L.Ed. 278, 282, 57 S.Ct. 255].)

(14) We have found that the evidence was sufficient to support a conviction for disturbing the peace by means of offensive conduct as prohibited by section 415 of the Penal Code. A decision which is right in result will not be reversed on appeal although the reason stated is wrong. (*People* v. *Evans,* 249 Cal.App.2d 254, 257 [57 Cal.Rptr. 276]; *People* v. *Selz,* 138 Cal.App.2d 205, 210 [291 P.2d 186].)

In a court trial, the trial judge's erroneous opinion on the law is not grounds for a reversal. (*People* v. *Wolfe,* 257 Cal.App.2d 420, 426 [64 Cal.Rptr. 855].) We have examined each of the points raised by the defendant without finding reversible error. The judgment is affirmed.

Roth, P. J., and Fleming, J., concurred.

Repouille v. United States; 165 F. 2d 152 (1947)

L. Hand, Circuit Judge

140   The District Attorney, on behalf of the Immigration and Naturalization Service, has appealed from an order, naturalizing the appellee, Repouille. The ground of the objection in the district court and here is that he did not show himself to have been a person of "good moral character" for the five years which preceded the filing of his petition.[1] The facts were as follows. The petition was filed on September 22, 1944, and on October 12, 1939, he had deliberately put to death his son, a boy of thirteen, by means of chloroform. His reason for this tragic deed was that the child had "suffered from birth from a brain injury which destined him to be an idiot and a physical monstrosity malformed in all four limbs. The child was blind, mute, and deformed. He had to be fed; the movements of his bladder and bowels were involuntary, and his entire life was spent in a small crib." Repouille had four other children at the time towards whom he has always been a dutiful and responsible parent; it may be assumed that his act was to help him in their nurture, which was being compromised by the burden imposed upon him in the care of the fifth. The family was altogether dependent upon his industry for its support. He was indicted for manslaughter in the first degree; but the jury brought in a verdict of manslaughter in the second degree with a recommendation of the "utmost clemency"; and the judge sentenced him to not less than five years nor more than ten, execution to be stayed, and the defendant to be placed on probation, from which he was discharged in December, 1945. Concededly, except for this act he conducted himself as a person of "good moral character" during the five years before he filed his petition. Indeed, if he had waited before filing his petition from September 22 to October 14, 1944, he would have had a clear

---

[1] § 707(a) (3), Title 8 U.S.C.A.

record for the necessary period, and would have been admitted without question.

[1, 2]   Very recently we had to pass upon the phrase "good moral character" in the Nationality Act;[2] and we said that it set as a test, not those standards which we might ourselves approve, but whether "the moral feelings, now prevalent generally in this country" would "be outraged" by the conduct in question: that is, whether it conformed to "the generally accepted moral conventions current at the time."[3] In the absence of some national inquisition, like a Gallup poll, that is indeed a difficult test to apply; often questions will arise to which the answer is not ascertainable, and where the petitioner must fail only because he has the affirmative. Indeed, in the case at bar itself the answer is not wholly certain; for we all know that there are great numbers of people of the most unimpeachable virtue, who think it morally justifiable to put an end to a life so inexorably destined to be a burden to others, and—so far as any possible interest of its own is concerned—condemned to a brutish existence, lower indeed than all but the lowest forms of sentient life. Nor is it inevitably an answer to say that it must be immoral to do this, until the law provides security against the abuses which would inevitably follow, unless the practice were regulated. Many people—probably most people—do not make it a final ethical test of conduct that it shall not violate law; few of us exact of ourselves or of others the unflinching obedience of a Socrates. There being no lawful means of accomplishing an end which they believe to be righteous in itself, there have always been conscientious persons who feel no scruple in acting in defiance of a law which is repugnant to their personal convictions, and who even regard as martyrs those who suffer by doing so. In our own history it is only necessary to recall the Abolitionists. It is reasonably clear that the jury which tried Repouille did not feel any moral repulsion at his crime. Although it was inescapably murder in the first degree, not only did they bring in a verdict that was flatly in the face of the facts and utterly absurd—for manslaughter in the second degree presupposes that the killing has not been deliberate—but they coupled even that with a recommendation which showed that in substance they wished to exculpate the offender. Moreover, it is also plain, from the sentence which he imposed, that the judge could not have seriously disagreed with their recommendation.

[2] § 707(a) (3), Title 8 U.S.C.A.
[3] United States v. Francioso, 2 Cir., 164 F.2d 163.

One might be tempted to seize upon all this as a reliable measure of current morals; and no doubt it should have its place in the scale; but we should hesitate to accept it as decisive, when, for example, we compare it with the fate of a similar offender in Massachusetts, who, although he was not executed, was imprisoned for life. Left at large as we are, without means of verifying our conclusion, and without authority to substitute our individual beliefs, the outcome must needs be tentative; and not much is gained by discussion. We can say no more than that, quite independently of what may be the current moral feeling as to legally administered euthanasia, we feel reasonably secure in holding that only a minority of virtuous persons would deem the practice morally justifiable, while it remains in private hands, even when the provocation is as overwhelming as it was in this instance.

[3]   However, we wish to make it plain that a new petition would not be open to this objection; and that the pitiable event, now long past, will not prevent Repouille from taking his place among us as a citizen. The assertion in his brief that he did not "intend" the petition to be filed until 1945, unhappily, is irrelevant; the statute makes crucial the actual date of filing.

Order reversed; petition dismissed without prejudice to the filing of a second petition.

Frank, Circuit Judge (dissenting)

This decision may be of small practical import to this petitioner for citizenship, since perhaps, on filing a new petition, he will promptly become a citizen. But the method used by my colleagues in disposing of this case may, as a precedent, have a very serious significance for many another future petitioner whose "good moral character" may be questioned (for any one of a variety of reasons which may be unrelated to a "mercy killing") in circumstances where the necessity of filing a new petition may cause a long and injurious delay.[1] Accordingly, I think it desirable to dissent.

The district judge found that Repouille was a person of "good moral character." Presumably, in so finding, the judge attempted to employ that statutory standard in accordance with our decisions, i.e., as measured by conduct in conformity with

---

[1] Consider, e.g., the case of a professional man, unable during a long delay, incident to his becoming a citizen, to practice his profession in certain states of this country.

"the generally accepted moral conventions at the time." My colleagues, although their sources of information concerning the pertinent mores are not shown to be superior to those of the district judge, reject his finding. And they do so, too, while conceding that their own conclusion is uncertain and (as they put it) "tentative." I incline to think that the correct statutory test (the test Congress intended) is the attitude of our ethical leaders. That attitude would not be too difficult to learn; indeed, my colleagues indicate that they think such leaders would agree with the district judge. But the precedents in this circuit constrain us to be guided by contemporary public opinion about which, cloistered as judges are, we have but vague notions. (One recalls Gibbon's remark that usually a person who talks of "the opinion of the world at large" is really referring to "the few people with whom I happened to converse.")

Seeking to apply a standard of this type, courts usually do not rely on evidence but utilize what is often called the doctrine of "judicial notice," which, in matters of this sort, properly permits informal inquiries by the judges.[2] However, for such a purpose (as in the discharge of many other judicial duties), the courts are inadequately staffed,[3] so that sometimes "judicial notice" actually means judicial ignorance.

But the courts are not utterly helpless; such judicial impotence has its limits. Especially when an issue importantly affecting a man's life is involved, it seems to me that we need not, and ought not, resort to our mere unchecked surmises, remaining wholly (to quote my colleagues' words) "without means of verifying our conclusions." Because court judgments are the most solemn kind of governmental acts—backed up as they are, if necessary, by the armed force of the government— they should, I think, have a more solid foundation. I see no good reason why a man's rights should be jeopardized by judges' needless lack of knowledge.

I think, therefore, that, in any case such as this, where we lack the means of determining present-day public reactions,

---

[2] Cf. Wigmore, *Evidence,* 3d Ed., §§ 41, 2569, 2571, 2580, 2583; Thayer, *A Preliminary Treatise On Evidence* (1898) 308–309; Davis, An Approach to Problems of Evidence in the Administrative Process, 55 *Harv. Law Rev.* (1942) 364, 404–405, 410; Morris, Law and Fact, 55 *Harv. Law Rev.* (1942) 1303, 1318–1325.

In this very case, my colleagues have relied on informally procured information with reference to "the fate of a similar offender in Massachusetts."

[3] Think how any competent administrative agency would act if faced with a problem like that before us here.

Cf. Frank, *If Men Were Angels* (1942) 122–127; L. Hand, J., in Parke-Davis & Co. v. H. K. Mulford Co., C.C., 189 F. 95, 115; Cohen, Benjamin Nathan Cardozo, 1 Nat. Lawyers Guild (1938) 283, 285; Morris, Law and Fact, 55 *Harv. Law Rev.* (1942) 1303, 1318–1319.

we should remand to the district judge with these directions: The judge should give the petitioner and the government the opportunity to bring to the judge's attention reliable information on the subject, which he may supplement in any appropriate way. All the data so obtained should be put on record. On the basis thereof, the judge should reconsider his decision and arrive at a conclusion. Then, if there is another appeal, we can avoid sheer guessing, which alone is now available to us, and can reach something like an informed judgment.[4]

---

[4] Of course, we cannot thus expect to attain certainty, for certainty on such a subject as public opinion is unattainable.

Commonwealth v. Donoghue; Court of Appeals of Kentucky, 1933; 250 Ky. 343, 63 S.W.2nd 3.

Stanley, Commissioner

The opinion deals with the sufficiency of an indictment charging the common-law offense of conspiracy, and relates to what are popularly referred to by the invidious and iniquitous term of "loan sharks." We shall abridge the indictment by omitting terms and words usually regarded as essential to technical sufficiency. The instrument charges M. Donoghue, W. T. Day, and Vernon L. Buckman with the offense of criminal conspiracy, committed as follows: That they unlawfully and corruptly conspired with one another and others, to the grand jury unknown, "to engage in the business of lending money in small amounts to poor and necessitous wage earners at excessive, exorbitant and usurious rates of interest and to prevent the recovery of such interest paid by said borrowers"; that while the conspiracy existed and in pursuance and furtherance thereof they "operated a money-lending business under the trade name of Boone Loan Company, with its office in Kenton County, Kentucky"; that the accused or one or more of them, with the advice, consent, and acquiescence of the others, acting in concert and in furtherance of the conspiracy and in the operation of the business did lend to hundreds of poor and necessitous wage earners small sums of money in amounts ranging from $5 to $50, at high, excessive, exorbitant, illegal, and usurious rates of interest, to wit, from 240 to 360 per cent per annum. Only Donoghue was before the court. The trial court sustained a demurrer to the indictment and dismissed it. The commonwealth has appealed. . . .

The comprehensiveness and indefiniteness of the offense of

conspiracy has made an exact definition a very difficult one, as has been stated. But the broad definition or description everywhere accepted is that conspiracy is a combination between two or more or persons to do or accomplish a criminal or unlawful act, or to do a lawful act by criminal or unlawful means. . . .

According to the overwhelming weight of authority the objects of the conspiracy need not be an offense against the criminal law for which an individual could be indicted or convicted, but it is sufficient if the purpose be unlawful. That term "unlawful" in this connection has been expanded beyond its original limits of being only some act punishable as a crime. . . .

So it may be said that within the contemplation of the offense of criminal conspiracy are the acts which by reason of the combination have a tendency to injure the public, to violate public policy, or to injure, oppress, or wrongfully prejudice individuals collectively or the public generally. . . .

With this abstract understanding as to what may be the subject-matter of a criminal conspiracy, we may direct our consideration to the subject of usurious demands and collections.

Now, the occupation of a usurer has been bitterly denounced in all ages of the civilized world, and in most Christian countries there have been laws to suppress it.

. . . It suffices to say that the business of the usurer has always called for vigorous condemnation and has ever been regarded as against public welfare and public policy. . . .

Our current statutes . . . merely declare that the portions of contracts calling for payment of interest in excess of 6 per cent are void, authorize the recovery of the excess, and require the lender in an action to avoid payment to bear the entire costs of the proceeding. . . . While in a degree this penalizes the usurer, the statute is remedial and cannot be regarded as making the act a criminal offense.

Turning our attention again to the indictment now before us. It is *much more* than merely a charge that the accused conspired to collect usury. The accusation is a conspiracy to carry on the business of lending money in small amounts from $5 to $50 to poor and necessitous wage-earners at rates of interest ranging from 240 to 360 per cent per annum, and then to prevent the recovery of the usury paid by such borrowers.

The indictment does not charge the accused with the mere exaction of usury, or with isolated instances of collecting slight excesses over the legal rate of interest. The objects of the conspiracy were not incidents to a legitimate business. If that were all, it might be doubted whether it could be regarded as an offense or an unlawful act within the meaning of that term in its relation to conspiracy. *It charges a nefarious plan for the habitual exaction of gross usury, that is, in essence, the operation of the business of extortion.* The import of the indictment is to charge systematic preying upon poor persons, of taking an unconscionable advantage of their needy condition, of oppressing them, of extorting money from them through the disguise of interest, and, as an intrinsic part of the plan, to prevent restitution by obstructing public justice and the administration of the law. If ever there was a violation of public policy as reflected by the statutes and public conscience, or a combination opposed to the commonweal, it is that sort of illegitimate business. It was extortioners of this class, called money changers, whom the Christ drove from the Temple on two occasions.

The amicus curiae filing brief on the appellee's side submits that the common-law offense of conspiracy of the sort charged is so indefinite and uncertain that it should not be recognized by the court. He would assimilate the view to the attitude of the courts under which are held invalid statutory laws that are so indefinite and uncertain as to be incapable of rational understanding or enforcement. We think the better comparison or analogy is to look upon the offense and the law as fraud, deceit, cheating and kindred wrongs are viewed. They are not capable of exact definition or delineation in the abstract, but when it comes to concrete considerations the courts have pretty well hammered the nebulous character of those wrongs into such shape as to make an offense recognizable. So, although in the abstract conspiracy of this sort must be loosely defined, an enlightened conscience should have no difficulty in recognizing a wrong as being embraced within its wide compass.

Measuring the indictment by the foregoing considerations, the court is of the opinion that it states a public offense.

Wherefore, the judgment is reversed.

Clay, J., dissenting

I am unable to concur in the majority opinion. However indefensible the exaction of usury may be, it is a matter that should be regulated by the Legislature and not by the courts. Already the conspiracy doctrine has been worked overtime, and should not be extended unless plainly required. When a court on the theory of conspiracy declares an act to be a crime, which was not recognized as a crime at the time it was done, its decision savors strongly of an ex post facto law.

The necessity of protecting the public, and particularly the laboring man, is much stressed, but that alone will not authorize the court to hold an indictment good. Moreover, it is not perceived how prosecutions like the one in question may help the situation as separate individuals may still continue the business of lending money at exorbitant rates without being subject to punishment.

The decision not only presents a strained application of the conspiracy doctrine, but its chief danger lies in the fact that for all time to come it will be the basis for the creation of new crimes never dreamed of by the people.

Bibliography

Durkheim, E. *The Division of Labor in Society* (translated by **149** George Simpson). New York: Free Press, 1933.

Gussfield, J. "On Legislating Morals," *California Law Review,* Vol. 56 (1968), p. 54.

Hart, H. L. A. *Law, Liberty and Morality.* Stanford, Calif.: Stanford University Press, 1963.

————. "Social Solidarity and the Enforcement of Morals," *Chicago Law Review,* Vol. 35 (1967), p. 1.

————. "The Use and Abuse of the Criminal Law," *Oxford Lawyer,* Vol. 4 (1961), p. 7.

Henkin, L. "Morals and the Constitution: The Sin of Obscenity," *Columbia Law Review,* Vol. 63 (1963), p. 391.

Hughes, G. "Morals and the Criminal Law," *Yale Law Journal,* Vol. 71 (1962), p. 662.

Kadish, S. "The Crisis of Overcriminalization," *Annals,* Vol. 374 (1967), p. 157.

Mewett, A. "Morality and the Criminal Law," *University of Toronto Law Journal,* Vol. 14 (1962), p. 213.

Mitchell, B. *Law, Morality and Religion in a Secular Society.* London: Oxford University Press, 1967.

Packer, H. *The Limits of the Criminal Sanction.* Stanford, Calif.: Stanford University Press, 1968.

"Private Consensual Adult Behavior: The Requirement of Harm to Others in the Enforcement of Morality," *U.C.L.A. Law Review,* Vol. 14 (1967), p. 581.

Rostow, E. "The Enforcement of Morals," *Cambridge Law Journal* (1960), p. 174. Reprinted in Rostow, E. *The Sovereign Prerogative.* New Haven, Conn.: Yale University Press, 1962.

Skolnick, J. "Coercion to Virtue," *Southern California Law Review,* Vol. 41 (1968), p. 588.

Stephen, J. *Liberty, Equality, Fraternity.* London: Smith, Elgard and Co., 1873.

Williams, G. "Sex and Morals in the Criminal Law," *Criminal Law Review* (1964), p. 253.

Wollheim, R. "Crime, Sin and Mr. Justice Devlin," *Encounter* (November 1959), p. 34.

Basic Problems
in Philosophy Series

A. I. Melden and Stanley Munsat
University of California. Irvine
General Editors

Morality and the Law
Richard A. Wasserstrom

Introduction   On Liberty, *John Stuart Mill*   Morals and the Criminal Law, *Lord Patrick Devlin*   Immorality and Treason, *H. L. A. Hart*   Lord Devlin and the Enforcement of Morals, *Ronald Dworkin*   Sins and Crimes, *A. R. Louch*   Morals Offenses and the Model Penal Code, *Louis B. Schwartz*   Paternalism, *Gerald Dworkin*   Four cases involving the enforcement of morality   Bibliography

War and Morality
Richard A. Wasserstrom

Introduction   The Moral Equivalent of War, *William James*   The Morality of Obliteration Bombing, *John C. Ford, S.J.*   War and Murder, *Elizabeth Anscombe*   Moral Judgment in Time of War, *Michael Walzer*   Pacifism: A Philosophical Analysis, *Jan Narveson*   On the Morality of War: A Preliminary Inquiry, *Richard Wasserstrom*   Judgment and Opinion, The International Tribunal, Nuremberg, Germany   Superior Orders, Nuclear Warfare, and the Dictates of Conscience, *Guenter Lewy*   Selected Bibliography